African American Philosophy and the African Diaspora

Series Editors

Jacoby Adeshei Carter
Department of Philosophy
John Jay College, CUNY
New York, New York, USA

Leonard Harris
Purdue University
West Lafayette, Indiana, USA

The *African American Philosophy and the African Diaspora* Series publishes high quality work that considers philosophically the experiences of African descendant peoples in the United States and the Americas. Featuring sing-authored manuscripts and anthologies of original essays, this collection of books advance the philosophical understanding of the problems that black people have faced and continue to face in the Western Hemisphere. Building on the work of pioneering black intellectuals, the series explores the philosophical issues of race, ethnicity, identity, liberation, subjugation, political struggles, and socio-economic conditions as they pertain to black experiences throughout the Americas.

More information about this series at
http://www.springer.com/series/14377

Jacoby Adeshei Carter

African American Contributions to the Americas' Cultures

A Critical Edition of Lectures by Alain Locke

palgrave
macmillan

Jacoby Adeshei Carter
Department of Philosophy
John Jay College, CUNY
New York, New York, USA

African American Philosophy and the African Diaspora
ISBN 978-1-137-52518-5 (hardcover)   ISBN 978-1-137-56572-3   (eBook)
ISBN 978-1-349-70711-9 (softcover)
DOI 10.1057/978-1-137-56572-3

Library of Congress Control Number: 2016951221

This Palgrave Macmillan imprint is published by Springer Nature
The registered company is Nature America Inc. New York
The registered company address is: 1 New York Plaza, New York, NY 10004, U.S.A.

With love, to Stephanie
With deepest gratitude, to Leonard Harris
To whom much is given, much is required

Acknowledgments

I must, of course, begin by thanking the Moorland-Spingarn Research Center at Howard University; their dedication to the preservation of not only Alain Locke's intellectual legacy, but many others, as well as to African American intellectual history is invaluable. I owe special thanks to Mrs. Joellen El Bashir, who was committed to supporting this project early on, and remained a powerful advocate all the way through, and my sincerest gratitude to the Interim Director Dr. Clifford Muse Jr. and all the staff. This project was supported in part by the Faculty Fellowship Publication Program of the City University of New York. I am indebted to the members of my writing group in that program, Suha Kudsieh, Isaac Xerxes Malki, Karen Shelby, Jacob Krammer, Lisa Pope Fisher, and our faculty mentor, Moustafa Bayoumi. I am extremely grateful to Jean Beauchamps and Joel Armstrong for their tremendous help in translating the second lecture.

I, of course, owe a tremendous debt of gratitude to my partner, Stephanie Browning, for her unfailing love and support, and who was always there to keep me focused and working to finish the book. Finally, I owe a debt of thanks to Leonard Harris, without whom this project would not have been possible, and who no doubt through the many conversations he had with me about the project made it better than it otherwise would have been.

CONTENTS

Introduction

The January 12, 2010, earthquake in Haiti devastated, but did not destroy, Haitian cultural riches. Haiti's cultural riches are both affective and physical. Resources for sustaining self-motivation in the face of travesty, as well as the paint, paper, stone, and wood afforded by the environment, are indomitable sinews of the cultural domain. It was the cultural riches of Haiti—its tradition of African inherited polyrhythm music, with its pentatonic scale, vibrant colors, magic, romantic, realist literature, and its self-confident, independent spirit—that Locke intended to study.

Alain Leroy Locke, the intellectual progenitor of the Harlem Renaissance, served from April 9 to July 10, 1943, as Inter-American Exchange Professor to Haiti under the joint auspices of the American Committee for Inter-American Artistic and Intellectual Relations and the Haitian Ministry of Education under the Haitian Presidency of Elie Lescot from whom he received the National Order of Honor and Merit. During his tenure as Inter-American exchange professor Locke delivered a series of six lectures collectively entitled *Le Rôle du Negre dans la Culture des Amériques*.[1] The theme of his variously titled lectures was "The Negro's Contribution to the Culture of the Americas." Throughout the lectures, Locke chronicles important contributions made by members of various Negro populations in the Americas to the art, literature, and culture of various American societies.

© The Editor(s) (if applicable) and The Author(s) 2016
J.A. Carter, *African American Contributions to the Americas' Cultures*, DOI 10.1057/978-1-137-56572-3_1

1

Locke received unexpected respect from his Haitian hosts during his frequent lectures. The landscape Locke observed in 1943 has undergone radical physical changes. Cultural and political change, ironically, were central features of Locke's lectures. A culture of democracy was coterminous with the success of democracy, best measured by the elimination of slavery's aftermath and the success of African cultural goods transplanted to the Americas. Pragmatism—the philosophical school with which Locke is most closely affiliated—has as an essential and pervasive concern the philosophical exploration not only of democracy as a system of governance but more importantly as a cultural pathos sufficient to constitute a way of life. The concern for the basic values and loyalties of democracy as well as the ways these are reflected in art as lived experience are driving concerns for pragmatists. In the year prior to the Haiti lectures Locke continued his work as one of the premier critical expounders of the virtues of African American artistic endeavors, while at the same time exploring philosophically the realities of intercultural encounters across racial and cultural lines, and the philosophical and practical significance of color and race as persistent impediments to the full realization of the democratic ideal nationally, regionally or on a global scale as manifest by his publication of the anthology *When Peoples Meet: A Study of Race and Culture Contacts*[2] co-edited with Bernhard J. Stern and guest editorship of a special issue of *Survey Graphic: A Magazine of Social Interpretation* entitled *Color: The Unfinished Business of Democracy*.[3] This body of work demonstrates that his philosophical work on democracy and art was well in advance of the leading pragmatist thinkers of his day, and much to our chagrin continues to outpace in many ways leading contemporary democratic theorists in terms of their neglect or willful blindness to issues of color.

When Locke became the American exchange professor to Haiti in 1943, he knew he was following in the footsteps of Frederick Douglass. Locke's residence in Haiti, however, had a different purpose. Locke devoted a great deal more time addressing the relationship of race and culture to democracy than was his original intent. Initially, he intended to study the African culture in Haiti, rightly or wrongly, he tended to associate its presence with the self-respect he championed against the self-deprecation wrought by slavery and racial discrimination. He was also focused on the historical issues of whether or not African traits survived slave making. Haiti, predominately Christian, also housed a panoply of African Gods as features of divination ceremonies as well as religious expressions; everywhere religious synergy was present. Locke was interested in examples of

West African cultural expression as evidence of ethnoracial continuums used for new creations, and such creative motifs for Locke were the *sine qua non* of a Renaissance. This project was partially lost in what became the lecture's dominant theme, namely, the meaning of democracy and the role of culture as a democratizing force.

The Haitian revolution against slavery was a central source of genuine democracy in the hemisphere and the index of democracy was a function of how Afrodescendant populations were treated in the hemisphere. Locke recommends a rapprochement between different forms of racism; the Anglo-Saxon form that created racial communities while denying individual rights, or the Latin form that applauded individual accomplishments and in so doing created a disparate racial community with race and class divisions. Locke advances a number of adventurous arguments as a function of answering a series of questions he began addressing in 1942 in "Who and What is Negro?," namely, "What makes a work of art Negro, its theme or its idiom? What constitutes a 'Negro contribution to culture,' its authorship or its cultural base? Is there or should there be any such set of categories in our critical thinking or our creative living?"[4] Such questions pose a challenge to the very practice and philosophy of culture, and the basis by which it can be justified and judged.

Locke graduated from Harvard University with a PhD in philosophy in 1918. He was a Rhodes Scholar at Oxford University, England, between 1907 and 1910, and pursued graduate study under Georg Simmel and Hugo Münsterberg at the University of Berlin, Germany, from 1910 to 1911. His career at Howard University, Washington, DC, began as an assistant professor of education, from 1912 to 1917 after which he became a professor of philosophy, from 1917 to 1954, receiving an Honorary Doctorate from Howard in 1953. Locke was a visiting professor at various universities: University of Wisconsin, Madison, 1945–1946; New School for Social Research, New York City, 1947; and City College of New York, 1948. He was a member of the American Negro Academy, American Philosophical Association, Associates in Negro Folk Education, International Institute of African Languages and Culture, League of American Writers, Society for Historical Research, Corresponding member of Académie des Sciences Colonailes, and honorary fellow of the Sociedad de Estudio Afro-Cubanos.

Long before his sojourn to Haiti, Locke's connections with the African world and issues of race began. He was on the Executive Committee of the Negro Academy in Washington founded by Alexander Crummel, and with

Arturo Alfonso Schomburg serving as president, and, in 1921, Locke spoke to the academy on "The Problem of Race and Culture." Locke returned to the Negro Academy in 1922 to speak on "The American Literary Tradition and the Negro," and in the following year on "Notes Made at Luxor, Egypt." In early 1924, the Society for Ethical Culture sponsored a three-day public conference on "Interracial Harmony and Peace." He joined, for example, the French Oriental Archaeological Society, Cairo, Egypt, in 1927, and attended meetings at the Institut d'Ethnologie de l'Université de Paris, in 1924. Locke sailed to Geneva around 1927 to study the Mandate system which was designed to protect the colonies. Locke prepared a report on the horror of forced labor in the Congo, but it was never accepted or published. Under King Leopold II, the Congo Free State was among the most brutal colonial regimes in human history, making mutilation and torture a daily feature to compel forced labor. Consequently, when Locke became the Inter-American Exchange Professor to Haiti, it followed a long history of work in the African world.

The New Negro, Locke's monumental opus, offered a new interpretation of African descendant peoples in the Americas. All conceptions and interpretations of a "New Negro" defined them as a population radically dissimilar from that population which created and sustained minstrelsy or its associated behaviors of self-effacement, subservience, and willingness to perform stereotypical roles evincing infantile emotions. The "New Negro" was self-confident, self-assured, and individually representative. Booker T. Washington's conservative conception of the "New Negro" was willing to accept segregation as a temporary condition in exchange for the opportunity to develop businesses and pursue higher education; patriotism and inclusion in the ideals, along with assimilation into the culture of the USA was the goal. Socialists conceived the "New Negro" as a working class agent of revolution, interested in the overthrow of capitalism, equality, and unity with white workers, forming progressive unions that enabled them to defend themselves. Marcus Garvey, leader of the Universal Negro Improvement Association, interpreted the "New Negro" in terms of conservative Christian moral values and dedicated to racial purity, racial uplift, and reunion with Africa. The National Association for the Advancement of Colored People's founder W.E.B. Du Bois conceived the "New Negro" as concerned with promoting non-violent protest, challenging the legal status of racial segregation and discrimination, and committed to the traditional moral virtues of the resident values in middle-class life in the USA. Locke held that a "New Negro" should be created roughly every half-generation or so; failure to do see represented an expressive stagnation, degeneration, or inhibition indicative of cultural decay. As for Locke, his version of the "New Negro" accentuated the aesthetic and affective dimensions of the rising artistic class of African Americans in the USA, African cultural retentions within those works, and the heterogeneity of African American expressions. Locke's ethics of self-formation and aesthetics of advocacy conflicted with all of the above conceptions and represented in his estimation a realization of possibilities denied to proponents of these earlier forms. It was his conception that sustained the Harlem Renaissance. In 1939, Locke recognized that he had too often focused on the "racial" element of the works of African American authors and that the renaissance was too often promoting its cultural activity as other than regional forms of expression. Nonetheless, it had helped the creation of the transformation of African American folk culture into forms of expressions that could be universally appreciated, and it had made African American folk culture far more appreciated as a source of culture products worthy of serious appreciation.

Arguably, public lectures in the nineteenth and early-twentieth centuries were far more important modes of communication than written works. Locke's lectures were transcribed and read but listened to attentively by far more people than likely read them. Only one of Locke's lectures was published in English and that too in a publication with a small circulation. Listening created an immediate impact and reading created an impact on successive readers at disparate times and distances. The memory of the audience, consequently, played a crucial role because they could not refer to the text to check or help recall the speaker's words. Rhetorical flourishes drew the listeners' attention. Shifts of emphasis in speeches give a different meaning than the written text, not just because of the difference in cognitive functions used by the brain to process the different forms of information; the form and its mode of presentation, consequently, effect what is conveyed.

Locke offers an insightful treatment of African descendant peoples in the Americas. On this particular point, his contribution is most pioneering, representing as it does a nearly six-decade advance on current pragmatist and American philosophical scholarship. Only recently have pragmatists—coming mostly from scholars also working in Latin American philosophy—begun to pay attention to the idea of the Americas as interconnected and interdependent regions also marked by diverse and divergent histories. The Americas are a region that shares common historical threads but that also diverges at important and interesting points. Chief among Locke's philosophical insights on this matter is his recognition that focusing on North America resulted in at best a myopic view of all of the Americas, or at worst a complete blindness to large portions of the Americas. Locke became increasingly suspect regarding the concepts of race and culture. Throughout his career, racialism and cultural provincialism seemed to Locke more and more divisive and at odds with the full incorporation on equal standing of Afrodescendant peoples into American cultures and American civilization. A diversity and plurality of types of culture seemed to him desirable and unavoidable. Cultural and racial chauvinism block the opportunities for democratic participation and collaboration.

Regrettably and undeniably underappreciated, the publication of this series of lectures provides an opportunity for renewed attention to Locke's philosophical contributions. From an Inter-American perspective, the novelty of his thought and the forward-thinking that characterizes his philosophical worldview open possible avenues of philosophical exploration that are sorely lacking in many contemporary philosophical circles. Arguably, the present state of scholarship in pragmatism, African American, and Africana philosophy suffer from unfamiliarity with the depth and breadth of Locke's thought. This volume seeks in part to remedy that dereliction.

NOTES

1. Locke's lectures on "The Negro's Contribution to the Culture of the Americas," delivered in Port-au-Prince, Haiti 1943 are in the Alain L. Locke Papers, Moorland-Spingarn Research Center, Howard University, 164-126/24 and in 164-126/4-29; these include the typescripts in English and in French, as well as a printed copy of "The Negro in the Three Americas" from the Journal of Negro Education (Winter 1944): 7–18. Publication is with the permission of the Moorland-Spingarn Research Center, Howard University.
2. Locke, Alain and Bernhard J. Stern, eds. When Peoples Meet: A Study in Race and Culture Contacts. Hinds, Hayden & Eldredge Revised edition, 1949.
3. Alain Leroy Locke, "The Unfinished Business of Democracy," Survey Graphic: Magazine of Social Interpretation, (1942), 31:11, 455–61.
4. Alain Leroy Locke, "Who, and What is Negro?" in *The Philosophy of Alain Locke: Harlem Renaissance and Beyond* edited by Leonard Harris, 209–228. Philadelphia: Temple University Press, 1989.

PART I

The Negro's Contribution to the Culture of the Americas

Lecture 1: Race, Culture, and Democracy

Madames, Messieurs

It is, I assure you, both a great pleasure and a great opportunity to be here on a mission of intercultural exchange. The mutual sympathy and understanding between Haiti, your country, and mine, the United States, closer than ever at present, can never be too close for mutual benefit. And I hope you will allow me to stress the phrase, 'mutual', for relations between countries and cultures, to be sound, constructive and self-respecting, must be two-way relations of give-and-take. The new order of the new day in human relations is reciprocity, not aggression, mutual assistance not over-lordship, fraternity, in short, not paternalism.

Fortunately during these recent years the relations of our two countries have been in the happy phase of reciprocity, as we now are able to realize they should always have been and as we all hope they will from now on continue to be. Enlightened nations today are beginning to see the larger significances of their institutional and cultural debts, of their common stakes in civilization rather than merely to count their territorial holdings and their balances of trade. To do so with consistency, however, requires a broad and humane perspective of history, with a good and honest memory, such as will balance, if I may illustrate concretely, the early and important assistance of Haiti to the United States during the Cornwallis campaign of our American Revolution with the much later payment in kind by our influential recognition of Haitian Independence; or later still, that welcome balancing of our moral accounts represented, on the one

© The Editor(s) (if applicable) and The Author(s) 2016
J.A. Carter, *African American Contributions to the Americas'*
Cultures, DOI 10.1057/978-1-137-56572-3_2

hand, by the 'Good Neighbor' treaty of 1934 and on the other, by Haiti's repayment in kind, her prompt and brave decision early in 1942 to declare war on the Axis Powers and to join the embattled cause of democracy.

In its small way, the present undertaking is also an integral part of the same happy and helpful reciprocity. On the one hand, there is the good initiative of The Committee on Inter-American Artistic and Intellectual Relations, under whose auspices I have the occasion to visit Haiti, and on the other, the deeply appreciated reciprocal courtesy of M. Dartigue and your Ministry of Public Education, under whose kind patronage I have the honor to deliver this series of lectures. I am happy and proud to be, for the moment, a small cargo of good will and mutual understanding borne on the tide of those two converging streams, that will in the future carry so much more intellectual commerce between Haiti and the United States, let us carefully note, in both directions. As a matter of fact, when I left my post at Howard University, from which institution I have, too, the honor of presenting you the most cordial fraternal greetings, your own distinguished scholar, M. Dantes Bellegarde, was happily functioning at our institution as an exchange professor in Latin-American History. It is appropriate, too, to acknowledge at this point another even more immediately helpful collaboration, that of an esteemed Haitian friend, Dr. Camille Lhérisson, who has added to an already treasured friendship a heavy but happy debt of gratitude by translating the English text of my English manuscript for this series of lectures. After it has suffered the discount of my inept accent, I may need to assure you that it is good, nay, masterful French, but you will appreciate nonetheless his considerable contribution to this and other projects of Haitian-American rapprochement.

However, I am sanguine about the purpose and propriety of my mission, particularly in view of the double bond of sympathy and interest between us; for we have, have we not, both the fellowship of democracy and that of the confraternity of race. Indeed, I scarcely know which of the two to emphasize, facing the agreeable alternative of saluting you either as fellow-Americans, in the best and generic sense of that term, or as comrades of race. Small matter, however, for it is my eventual purpose to tie the two together, having chosen as my general subject: *The Negro's Contribution to the Culture of the Americas*. In this way I hope to be able to make North American culture a little better understood and appreciated, and especially that part of it which has been vitally influenced by the American Negro. Also, though I hasten to confess myself less competent in this field, it is my purpose to show how importantly and strategically this Negro and originally African segment of culture exists as a common denominator, little known but quite historic and fundamental, between some of the most important national cultures of the Americas. For certainly in many places in North, Central and South America, including the variegated cultures of the Caribbean, Negro idioms and traditions have added vitality and flavor to art, music, dance, drama and folklore, and entered so deeply into the matrix of these cultures as to make it impossible for them to be eliminated or ignored.

Indeed, as our American cultures come into closer contact and understanding this will become increasingly apparent. Ultimately this linkage of a common indebtedness to African and Negro elements of culture may well introduce an important new spiritual dimension into our inter-American unity, and help develop among and between us the full potential of social and cultural democracy.

How can we hope to achieve cultural democracy unless we extend the formula of equality and fraternity across the boundaries and barriers of both race and nationality, to comprehend not merely the basic relations of persons within our several groups but also the relationships of groups themselves to one another? The parity of nations, races, and cultures is, in my opinion, the next and necessary step in the evolution of the democratic ideal. We shall not achieve this on the political plane successfully unless it is reinforced by a moral and spiritual conviction that this is the foundation principle of just and enduring group relations, and such a spiritual faith can only arise from the transformation of those provincialisms, which narrow unnecessarily our traditional conceptions of ourselves, still rooted in our various cultures. The mainstay of our pride in them is by reason of their exclusiveness and asserted superiorities. We shall see later how contrary to fact these superstitions of culture really are. We have, it is true, a certain obvious distinctive character in our several cultures, and probably always will have them. But in the really more important factors of our culture,—Christianity, democratic institutions, modern industrial technology, science and scientific method, the logic of thought and reason, the basic art forms, the fundamental aesthetic and moral reactions, are common to us all. Their national aspects are primarily matters of particular emphasis and flavor. We have also, in addition to this common civilization, a basic solidarity of interests which we must learn to recognize, appreciate, mature, and promote. Only cultural parochialism stands between us and this larger perspective; and when we finally outgrow such subjective limitations, a new panorama of the past and of the future of mankind will open out before our enlightened eyes.

As the fog of chauvinism lifts from the language of history, we shall finally realize that for nearly a century and a half we have been victims of a political conception of culture, inappropriate, undemocratic, and inhumane. Earlier centuries, in spite of other lacks, had a truer and greater outlook on the world. Medieval Europe had its grand over-concept of Christendom: the Renaissance, equally universal in a secular way, had its humanism uniting all Europe culturally without regard to nationality; and in the cosmopolitan Eighteenth Century, so close were the intellectual and cultural relations both of France with England and with Germany, and they in turn with the Lowland Countries, that men were scarcely conscious of that great divide which we know today as the dichotomy of the Anglo-Saxon and Latin thought and feeling. Strange but true, that as our world has enlarged and our intercommunications immeasurably improved, our conception of culture and human solidarity has narrowed and shrunk. Yet just so, has nationalism, in the nineteenth and early-twentieth centuries, beclouded our view of the true facts of culture history and excluded from all but a few more scientifically minded among us, the wider and more humane notions of human kinship. Let us not chide the Nazi or Japanese racialists with the blame for the totalitarian concept of culture and nationality and the master-race interpretation of history. For we, too, have subconsciously at times openly held modified forms of the same characteristic notions. We too, have believed that culture and race were somehow organically related and that civilization was both the sole product and property of those classes, nations or ethnic groups that have sat in the seat of political and economic power. The facts are all to the contrary. Some of the richest growths of culture have been transplanted crops not native to the land in which they flowered; some of the finest idioms of the arts, music, dance and folklore especially, have come from lowly peasant stocks, often alien peasant-folk at that: a great deal of what is best in culture derives not from pure but from crossed and hybrid strains which seem to be enriched by this process of cultural cross-fertilization. Incidentally, but importantly, the cultural products of the Negro in all parts of the Americas where he has been in considerable numbers have demonstrated and exemplified these basic truths about the nature of culture, traditional opinions notwithstanding. Indeed long before modern anthropology came along to correct our thinking on these matters, the practical results of Negro creative interaction with both Anglo-Saxon and Latin elements of American culture has demonstrated, to any eye that would see clearly, the same conclusions.

Here in this instance we have the spiritual products of the lowliest folk becoming a dominate force in certain areas of a country's culture; indeed as in the case with Negro musical idioms in the United States and Brazil providing the major component in what has come to be accepted as the nationally characteristic idiom. This is not an isolated instance; it could be cited on several other scores and with reference to many other nations both with respect to the cultural influence of the Negro and that of the American Indian. The tradition, as I have already pointed out, has not been favorably set for us to learn the obviously important democratic lesson involved in such situations, but these lessons are there, like Shakespeare's silent "sermons in stones," to be eventually recognized. Indeed if we would truly democratize our culture, we must learn them. We might even go so far as to say that our culture had been more democratic than we ourselves have been.

But today, from both scientific and practical angles it is being brought home to us that civilization is not the product of a single people, and that all great national cultures are composite in character and derivation. In the long run we shall probably discover this as, in the realm of social ideas, the one great spiritual lesson stemming from the chastening and clarifying ordeal of the present world crisis. When that time comes democracy will be more than a political formula; it will be a living faith and spirit of human brotherhood; a firm creed and conviction of human interdependence. We are still far from a general recognition of this; however.

One may well stop at this point to consider why. American thinking, generally weaned from colonial dependence by now, has nevertheless retained, it seems, one lingering colonial trait. It follows the European cult of nationalism and the traditional European identification of nationality with culture. We have all projected this political pattern on our several national lives, hardly realizing what a misfit it is. For the typical American state, whether of North or South America, is both multi-racial and multi-national in its human and cultural composition. In America, we are Switzerlands, only even more intermingled.

These newer nations have no need or reason to make the mistake of projecting Old World patterns and traditions upon an essentially new type of culture. By so doing they not only belie their own basic structure but postpone the development of their potentialities as pioneers of that cosmopolitan culture typical of complete democracy and of an increasingly international world. To realize the obscuring force of the national myth in the realm of culture, one needs only stop a moment to contrast with the actual facts the oversimplified notion, for example, of the culture of the United

States as exclusively or predominantly Anglo-Saxon. Need one refer to its medley of peoples and races, its flourishing foreign language press and periodicals,—some non-English newspapers, and more significant even, its mélange of traditions and cultural elements, among which the Negro element has its weighty and now acknowledged share. Or again, we can refer to the same traditional illusion of cultural uniformity about bilingual Canada, with its more than dual culture, if we include, as we should, that of the Canadian Indian. So, political conventions to the contrary, we have few if any monotype cultures in the Western hemisphere: it is not the typical or predominant American pattern. So we must build our several national societies on actual American realities, not on outworn European stereotypes. Accordingly, if we would face the fertile future rather than the stagnant and sterile past, particularly if we would avoid the old clashes and enmities of arrogant and competitive nationalism, we American nations must mold ourselves on the formula of national units that embrace and prize and integrate cultural diversity, weaving many strains of culture into a richer and harmonious pattern of a composite civilization. Only in this way can we reconcile our valued and still valuable political nationalism with the oncoming cultural internationalism.

More than this; there are national problems too which can only be solved by a similar formula. For only in this way can we fruitfully merge cultural elements that migration and the accidents of history have jux-taposed within our several national boundaries. Traditionally hostile or incompatible with one another, here they are represented in our mixed populations by considerable segments of loyal descendants. Hitherto, they have met in a sort of truce of democratic convenience or mutual indiffer-ence. It is high time now, especially since we need a more vital solidarity within democracy and between the democracies, that this truce be worked through to real cultural concord and understanding. In the United States this relatively new philosophy of society and culture is being described as and promoted as "cultural pluralism." It is, a promising creed and already has many powerful intellectual and scientific adherents. I should like to commend it as the only fully democratic notion of culture and the only realistic and safe concept of nationality. For the majority factions, it imposes modesty, tolerance and a fraternal spirit; for the minority groups it is a boon of protection, self-respect and reciprocity.

Already under its influence, in the United States, and still more delib-erately in Mexico, the culture of the American Indian is being completely revalued. It is no longer being regarded as a despised and isolated folk culture, alien to that of the educated elite, but rather as something which, in addition to being a precious heritage of those who are its direct descendants, has contributed to the general culture, and has possibilities, when properly appreciated and developed, of making further contributions. The same is true of the enlightened contemporary view of the Negro's folk culture in North America, and the parallel movement for a higher evaluation of the Afro-Cuban, the Afro-Brazilian, and the Afro-Antillean factors in their respective regional cultures is part of the same tendency. There is a democratic lesson for all our societies in such ideas and their reversal of old values. The old aristocratic notion of higher and lower culture, stratified according to social tradition, is thus being replaced by a more democratic conception of interacting group cultures, with cultural superiority determined only in particular instances by the force and direction of the creative influence. And never, let us add, cultural superiority or inferiority in general.

An especially illuminating case is that of the North American Negro. Here because of the Negro's adoption of the language and religion of the dominant majority, there was even less separation of culture between the two groups. Nevertheless there has been a strong counter-influence on the part of the Negro minority. Though disparaged socially and economically, and disadvantaged in formal culture, many distinctive and idiomatic traits in our racial tradition and expression have had very considerable influence on the general culture. This is quite generally known and admitted with respect to the marked Negro role in the formation of a characteristic American type of music, but it is equally true of many other cultural fields,—dance, drama, folk-lore and art, as these lectures will point out in due course. What concerns us primarily, for the moment, however, is the general lesson in the situation of a handicapped minority becoming culturally influential despite such handicaps. As often before in human history an oppressed minority has exerted spiritual power and become a dominant cultural force.

To some it may seem a paradox that certain of the most representative aspects of American culture should derive from the folk-life and folk-spirit of the humbler and more disadvantaged element of the population. But there is a deep and sufficient,—and we must add, a universal reason. It is only because, even in being characteristically racial, these creative expressions have also been basically and universally human, and have thus obtained a contagious and irresistible hold upon human sympathy and understanding. Let us try to illustrate this concretely, and perhaps at the same time track down the paradox that seems to underlie it. Everyone will admit that the American Negro Spiritual is a case in point, and no one will care to deny that it is a unique and priceless genre of creative musical expression. Here it is, on the one hand unmistakably racial, but on the other, deeply human and universal; in some respects typically and characteristically Negro, in others representatively American.

Interpretation of the "spirituals" has divided critical opinion into two opposing schools of thought, two critical camps between whose contending claims we are often disposed to give up the issue with a Shakespearean curse: "A plague on both your houses!" The racialists point out the obvious Negro idioms of song, imagination, and speech; the spirituals they say are Negro through and through; they mirror the Negro soul; the spirituals are black. Another group of critics, in a minority, but not for that matter, wrong, point out, with considerable warrant of fact that the spirituals are dialect folk-versions of Anglo-Saxon, Christian worship, taken over by ear and word of mouth from the King James Bible and Protestant evangelical hymns by the illiterate, converted slaves. The framework and substance of the Spirituals, these partisans say, is Anglo-Saxon and colonial American, and so, except for the tincture of Negro dialect and song, the spirituals are "white".

There is a great fallacy at the heart of this controversy. The Negro spiritual, like much else in the realm of art, has two parent cultures. It is a rare and rich culture hybrid, a unique and distinct Afro-American product, explainable only in terms of its dual inheritance. From the Negro side, it distills a racial temperament and a quite peculiar folk experience and fuses it with the great tradition of Protestant Christianity, stemming from the Nordic side. The composite blend transcends its individual ingredients in that alchemy of great creative art which Browning describes as the magic which "makes out of three sounds, not a fourth sound, but a star." Proof of this is the timeless and deep human universality that makes these songs common spiritual currency circulating everywhere at par and with immediate, almost spontaneous acceptance. As a synthesis of several strands of human experience, as effectively reaching down to common denominators of human emotion, the Negro spiritual has broken through the bonds of that which is provincially racial, though remaining, at the same time racially representative because of its special idiom and flavor. The true facts of the situation, therefore, justify no chauvinism of race and make it foolish to engage in partisan culture politics over fusions of culture which are so obviously sound and productive and in which, as in physical fatherhood and motherhood, both cultures play an essential role.

For a period, it is true, it was necessary to emphasize the Negro claims, because of the traditional disparagement of the black minority and their cultural possibilities by the dominant white majority. Confronting the Nordic egotisms of race, a counter-assertion of racial pride and credit was an inevitable human reaction. Negro critics had to justify the Negro's unnoticed role in American culture. But now that this role has been definitely recognized, it is time for a broader, more objective estimate of interaction of the two elements in our American culture, much of whose distinctiveness has come about only as a direct result of the union of two such diverse temperaments and traditions. But diverse as they are, the black and white cultures have in their artistic union been singularly productive and compatible. They have cross-fertilized to produce some of the most characteristic culture of this hemisphere.

Nor has this artistic productiveness been a one-generation crop, or a matter of the past. It is giving richer yield as time goes on, particularly as the Negro culture matures beyond the stage of folk art to the levels of more formal development. This, too, was once mistakenly conceived. It was thought that the liaison of the two cultural strains that existed in the folk art period of slavery was fruitful, but that the more formal marriage of the traditions would be barren. The use and development of Negro idioms and themes in our contemporary art by both white and Negro creative artists definitely proves the contrary. In fact, the more native and original our American arts become, the more prominent and fruitful do these non-European elements seem to be. Dudley Fitts, in his foreword to his *Anthology of Contemporary Latin American Poetry* rightly says: In the new poetry of our generation, "[n]ative themes and native rhythms—whether Indian, Afro-Antillean or Gaucho—have energized it, transforming it into something that is peculiarly American and wholly of our own time. It has never lost the profound tones of its European ancestry, but it speaks to us with a voice that is authentically its own. Poetry, after long absence, has returned to the people"[1] (Fitts, xi). The same can be said of the most virile and original trends in our North American art. Here, too, the elements credited with native flavor to our contemporary art stem in great part from the minority cultures: the Indian, the Negro, the other than Anglo-Saxon stocks. Crafted upon the roots of the old majority culture, these newer, less sophisticated cultures rejuvenate it, bringing a fresh vitality that makes the new art more distinctive and at the same time more representative. Our artists have learned, it seems, that only out of more democratic art can we achieve a more characteristic and American art.

It is worth more than passing notice that Dudley Fitts, whom we have just quoted, in mentioning the leading pioneers of this more indigenous American poetry sees fit to name Nicolas Guillen, the mixed-blood leader of the Afro-Cuban school of poetry, Alejandro Peralta, the Peruvian-Indian, and together with your own Jacques Roumain and that distinguished precursor, champion of native traditions, Duraciné Vaval. To whom, from my own point of view, as knowing the necessity of a background of scholarship for all such art movements, would add the name of my distinguished friend, Dr. Price Mars.

But it is not merely or only a matter of Haitian letters: the significant thing is the similarity of trend, coming from independent national cultures and from all sides. To Guillen, for example, who is characterized as the "genius who brought the *son*," the local Cuban folksong, into literature and who made African folklore, which is still current in the Antilles, popular as artistic material, we, in the United States can add our counterparts. For we have Langston Hughes, whose novel artistry derives from the idioms and rhythms of the "blues"; and Sterling Brown another of our best younger poets, whose work reflects the folk-ballad inspiration of the contemporary Negro peasant and city-proletarian. Not only has the poetry come back to the people; the people are making their gifts, and rich ones at that—to art.

In the past, we have felt that the use of folk materials in art meant stepping down to the level of primitive illiteracy and to the half-articulate, limited language of dialect. We now know that no such condescension is necessary or desirable. On the contrary, we now recognize that formal art has lessons to learn from folk-art in the very process of re-working its materials over into a new creation which is a synthesis of both the academic and the naïve, of folk culture with cosmopolitan culture. And so, it is a marriage rather than a misalliance which our progressive artists and thinkers are proposing between the two, and which many of them in their new art successfully consummate. In Haiti, if I may venture the opinion, such a cultural program has vast possibilities. Already there is underway,—at least so it seems to an outsider, a promising program for the artistic and intellectual union of your two constituent cultures,—the old, ancestrally African maternal culture of the hills with the paternal French culture, in which you have always been so adept, and of which you are so justly proud. If, as it would seem in the light of contemporary experience all over the hemisphere, the joining of cultures is a happy and fruitful union, one can then predict reliably for the near future a great upsurge of creative originality in Haitian culture. It may well be, too, that in the course of increasingly close relationships with the United States, a profitable cultural interchange will take place additionally between cultural traditions too often regarded as incompatible. I have already referred to the historical facts that contradict this superstition of incompatibility between Anglo-Saxon and Latin cultures; so one need only mention in passing such evidence as the close cultural bonds of France and England in the Eighteenth Century, or, for that matter, the monumental evidence of the English language itself, with its heavy admixture of Latin-French. History itself, then, says that it can happen again.

Since this was written, as though to supply my thesis with an apt and significant contemporary illustration, an event of international cultural significance has transpired; one which incidentally has given Haitians and the friends of Haiti the deepest feeling of satisfaction and pride. It is an event on which I consider it an honor to be able to offer the talented young authors and their proud compatriots my heartiest congratulations. I refer, or course, to the award of the Pan-American literature prize to Messrs. Phillipe et Pierre Thoby-Marcelin for their novel of Haitian life. Here we have a concrete and convincing illustration of what I have been discussing, of the way by which, when raised to the plane of formal art and universalized expression, that which was merely local and national can be made to acquire international significance and influence, and still also remain in substance racially representative. Because of course one instantly recognizes that in the case of this award the significance is as intimately national and racial as it is international and human, thanks to the fact that these young writers have chosen, wisely, not to flee to an ivory tower of colorless cosmopolitanism but, on the contrary, have dug deep into the human soil of this city and transmitted the life of their immediate environment into a flower of such universal beauty and significance that it, at the same time that it enriches the art and culture of the American continent, it makes Haiti known as a nation and the Negro people better appreciated as a source of distinctive and vital contemporary culture.

Indeed our best notion of what may happen in these matters is not even in the remote past, but in certain obvious contemporary happenings. To date the most concrete case in point is in the field of contemporary American music. In almost every country of the hemisphere where there has been a worthwhile musical development a similar sequence has occurred. As long as the musical tradition was basically European and only "classical" in the academic sense of that term, the music has remained derivative, imitative and provincial in spite of its cosmopolitan pretensions.

Once the composers turned to native idioms and folk materials, a strong and freshly creative stream of originality has been tapped. One need only mention Roldan, Caturla, Lecuona for Cuba, Chavez for Mexico, Villa-Lobos, Fernandez, and Mignone for Brazil. In the United States, the triumph of folk idioms in the works of Aaron Copland, Roy Harris, George Gershwin, including the works of the Negro composer William Grant Still, prove the case with considerable point. After dominating for several generations now our popular music and dance, the Negro musical idioms have begun the conquest of the Parnaessus of formal music and are having an almost dominant share in the creation in the United States of a characteristic American musical tradition and style.

Although manifested earlier and more strongly in music, this trend has definitely spread to most of the other arts—poetry, dance, drama, painting, sculpture, [and] creative prose. Apart from the Negro creative talents whose work will be analyzed more fully in later lectures, one need only mention as examples of this wide influence of Negro materials in the various arts such recognized names among North American contemporaries as Ridgley Torrence, Eugene O'Neill, Pail Green and DuBose Heyward in drama, Vechell Lindsay, Sanburg and Stephen Bennet in poetry, Julie Peterkin, Heyward, William Maron, Hamilton Besso Erskine Caldwell in fiction, Julius Bloch, James Chapin, Thomas Benton, Charles Shannon in painting, Harkavy, Hovannes, Malvina Hoffman, and others in sculpture.

We have, of course, our own significant creative racial talents in all these fields, but I am mentioning for the moment only a sample few of those white creative artists who in the United States have adopted Negro themes and idioms as frequent and sometimes preferred modes of their own most serious artistic expression. This is a cultural phenomenon of the first magnitude: in fact, it is cultural democracy in the making, and as far as art has a social influence, a strong force for greater democracy in the other more practical relations of life. With increasing frequency and with growing sympathy and spiritual penetration, such artists and their art are projecting Negro life as an integral and fully respected part of the national scene. In marked contrast with the superficial, trivial and condescending treatment of Negro materials which was, with few exceptions, fairly general, as late as a half-generation back, this represents a significant advance. By means of it, we may say, without fear of contradiction, that the Negro culture is today regarded as an essential ingredient of our Native American art and the Negro artist accepted as a recognized collaborator in its development rather than merely as a folk exponent or minority spokesman.

This notion of a collaboration between the white and the Negro artist is perhaps the most significant aspect of the whole development. It signals the elimination of narrow racialism at least from the philosophy of the art world, and substitutes for the partisanships of cultural politics the unifying bonds of a common cause. It is a humane and democratic condition when a non-Negro creative artist becomes by voluntary emphasis of interest and projected sympathy an exponent of Negro art. "Negro art" then comes to stand neither for a Ghetto for the Negro artists nor an exotic pastime for the white artist, but a common field of labor in the cultivation of a nationally typical art. Let us hope that in this, in addition to being pioneers of a more vital and inclusive art, our artists prove also to be prophets of a broader and more consistent democracy in the society at large.

Of one thing we may be sure:—once they are generally recognized these newer cultural attitudes will transform the meaning of race in art. Instead of being a label of lowly and provincial origin, it will be a hallmark of national flavor and character: instead of being the voice of a nation within a nation, it will be merely one of the many themes woven into the harmonious pattern of the national culture. At the outset of the evening, I expressed the hope that it would be possible to bring you in one and the same report an account of the intellectual and artistic progress of the Negro in the United States that would also represent the progress and development of our national culture in general. This forecast, I hope, has been fulfilled. I would by no means imply that in my country we have reached either the fullest possible democracy or the millennium of interracial relations. For indeed we have not, which measures just how much more work remains to be done on the growing edifice of democratic society. But at least it is a deep satisfaction to be able to report that stones once rejected and cast aside have become cornerstones in the up building of our national culture. To this extent, at least, democracy has been gloriously vindicated. Like the small nation, the racial or cultural minority are practical touchstones of spiritual integrity in a democracy. Cultural democracy is therefore a necessary intellectual and moral foundation for any other sort of democratic relationships, as the French founders so clearly foresaw when they linked the spirit of fraternity with the more concrete and practical principles of liberty and equality. To the extent that we promote this spirit within and between our various American nations, we shall be adding to the framework of our democratic institutions this indispensable spiritual breath and life-blood.

Permit me (it is Sunday) a concluding text and lesson in this matter of culture and democracy. In his admirable discourse of last week, Dr. Laubach quoted your sous-ministre of Foreign Affairs in a well-deserved tribute to the great mass of the Haitian people, saying "We won our independence in Creole." True as that is, there is something even more true that in conclusion, I presume to call to your attention.

Your historic independence was won by a happy union of elements,— the mass force and loyalty of the common people led and inspired; however, by the ideology of the French Revolution. Of this you have a constant and revered reminder, certainly, in your national motto: "L'Union Fait la Force." May I suggest that it has a meaning beyond the political, and in the field of our discussion? Full democracy and a truly democratic culture for Haiti, as indeed for our whole American hemisphere hinges on the application of this principle to our lives today. That means for you, the nearer approach and understanding between the town and the country, the French and the creole, a closer collaboration of the elite and the masses. For us, in the United States it means, a fuller solidarity among all our constituent stocks, and especially between black and white. For all of us, it must mean a better understanding and closer cooperation between those of Latin and those of Anglo-Saxon culture, between full-blood and mixed-blood, Negro, Indian, Asiatic and Euro-American, between North America, South America and the Caribbean. Out of such unity must come democracy's future force.

NOTE

1. Fitts, Dudley. "Preface," in *Anthology of Contemporary Latin American Poetry*, edited by Dudley Fitts and Hoffman Reynolds Hays, Norfolk: New Directions Press, 1942.

Lecture 2: The African Heritage and Its Cultural Significance

There is a great historical dilemma that for generations has troubled the Negro mind and spirit and divided the ways of Negro thinking. It is the conflict between a deep-seated emotional love and pride of race and an equally deep-rooted intellectual shame and distaste of race. This dilemma, we recognize immediately as the after-effect of slavery, which first rudely cut Negroes off from their ancestral African cultures and then taught them to ignore or despise their racial past without as much as a good look at it to see whether it merited such neglect and condemnation. It has taken more than two centuries to discover the intellectual correctives for this error, the proper antidote for this cultural poison. In saying this, I do not over-look the steady persistence underneath or the brave outcroppings now and then of pride of race among us. Perhaps I should also add that Haiti, with its proud tradition of self-emancipation and of nearly a hundred and fifty years of political independence, has been less affected by this psychologi-cal aftermath of slavery than any other American group of African descent. Certainly, one must call attention to the fact that generally speaking, and even sometimes in Haiti, Africa and things African have been misunder-stood and disparaged for lack of proper understanding of their cultural significance. So, by and large, we have been at a loss to implement our pride of race, to give it proper force and authority, to supply it with sober and intelligent directives. Thus, long after the physical ills and handicaps of slavery ceased, the psychological blight and stigma of it has persisted. It has conditioned among most groups of African Negro ancestry, a nega-

© The Editor(s) (if applicable) and The Author(s) 2016   23
J.A. Carter, *African American Contributions to the Americas'*
Cultures, DOI 10.1057/978-1-137-56572-3_3

tive rather than a positive regard for their racial past and their own cultural roots and origins. Some have contended that even if this past were worthwhile, it was now too late to salvage and reconstruct it; others, even more under the influence of what has aptly been called "the myth of the Negro past," have regarded that past as of little or no value. All of which has been tragic, because both contentions are wrong and in due course of time must definitely be counteracted.

All of the constituent American stocks except the American Indian, and maybe not even that exception, our latest anthropology suggest—are transplanted groups who by new adoptions and assimilations have become both hybrids and changelings of culture. The Euro-American has not found it necessary or desirable to renounce his European cultural heritage, just as the European, in turn, did not find it profitable to repudiate his pagan, his primitive or his barbarian past. Whether this background is Scandinavian, Slav, Teutonic, Anglo-Saxon, Celtic or Latin, it has always remained a vital and precious inheritance. They persist in his cultural tradition, particularly as a heritage of art and folklore, yielding constant spiritual dividends. It has not been found necessary, in giving up paganism, to blot out knowledge or respect for the pagan past. And as for ourselves, neither in piety nor in ignorance should we voluntarily continue in ways of thinking which slavery forced upon us in order to dominate the mind as well as shackle the body.

Fortunately this spiritual enslavement is ending. Another generation or so of careful scholarship and the African past will have been formidably resurrected. The net result, if it were the hard work of real scholarship and not race demagoguery, should neither snare us in primitivism nor wall us up in racial chauvinism. On the contrary, it will open up for us a normal and wholesome historical perspective and restore our temporarily obscured segment of human history.

The reconstruction of our group history, racially motivated but objective and above reproach as far as scholarship is concerned, has been one of the outstanding achievements of the last two decades in the intellectual life of Negroes in the United States. Our two senior scholars, Dr. Du Bois and Dr. Carter Woodson, have pioneered in this and both have insisted on the special importance of restoring the lost African chapters in that history. Younger scholars have taken up the undertaking in greater and more specialized detail, and there has additionally come to the aid of the movement the new materials and techniques of anthropology. One need only mention such names as those of E. Franklin Frazier, Melville Herskovits,

Morton Kahn, George Simpson, Harold Courlander, Zora Neale Hurston, Maurice Delafosse, Fernando Ortiz, Arthur Ramos, Gilberto Freyre, and your own Price Mars and J. C. Dorsainvil, to realize that this, too, is a task of wide and happy collaboration among scholars of all nations and races interested in the reconstruction of the African past.

Oddly enough, some of the best clues, have come from the comparative study of African continuity in the New World, for in spite of the wide dispersion of the slave trade and the many different strains of cultural assimilation, which Negro groups have been subject to, there are traceable survivals. In the mosaic pieced together by these observations in West Africa, South and Central America, the Southern United States, especially the coastal islands and here and there throughout the Caribbean, anthropologists are able to see beyond mere minutiae of stagnant tribal folk-ways a more or less common denominator culture that may reliably be considered typically African. Africa, for all its extreme and bewildering diversities, has after all no wider ones than Continental Europe. Indeed, Africa has less, if West and Equatorial Africa are taken as the basis of what we shall call typically African. We find certain basic characteristics meaningful for comprehending European civilization and culture; and we need similar broad characterizations for the proper evaluation of what we shall regard as representatively Negro.

Experts have already been able to trace, in music and folklore, the broad lines of similar common denominators. It remains only to identify the most complex political legacies, including those who have some social and spiritual importance, by thoroughly studying African continuity that cultural traditions are sure to indicate, and comparing them with the ancestral cultures. Because we know that deep-seated traits survive, despite the brutality and violence of exploitation such as American slavery, and that neither the loss of a language nor a radical transformation of religion and way of life can sufficiently destroy what existed originally in cultural life, and that is transmitted unconsciously, from one generation to another. Naturally, this is purely social, and not biological in its transmission. Sometimes so segmental, other times as a remarkably integrated network, African traits have survived: a distinctive state, a musical motif, a popular, persistent social attitude or belief, an emotional reaction, a typical element in the decor or clothing, a rite of mundane but steady appearance. These different elements dispersed from bottom to top, from the islands of Georgia's coast to Pernambuco, Dahomey and Guinea, to the mountains of Haiti and the villages of the Bahamas, the rituals of the Yoruba

Voodoo magic of Bahia, Gonaives and New Orleans; the Ivory Coast to the jungles of Surinam. All these phenomena demonstrate the tenacious hold of popular culture, even among groups who have lost contact with their language, their history and their popular beliefs.

For a long time, such facts have formed the curiosity for anthropological technique and folklore. However, now that the evidence is mounting, a more general phenomenon of interest and of great importance emerges. What was at first vague, becomes increasingly clear, and what is typically African or Negro is basically accurate. I can give a concrete illustration by indicating what we are starting to know of African music, now that we can trace its various branches and variants, placing them one next to the other, as would the botanist, to compare branches to the roots. Similarities in rhythm, in cadence, tone intervals between Afro-Brazilian popular songs, Afro-Cuban, Afro-Antillean, and Afro-American, have provided researchers with their initial evidence, the means to do better analysis of music of West African tribes, and these have in turn provided a basis which, for the first time, convincingly explains some common characters of American variants. These fundamental characteristics were previously obscured by superficial differences, which seem to be less important now that we know them. We are able to see that, after being mixed here with French musical themes, there with Spanish themes, and in other circumstances, with Anglo-Saxon themes, and even with mixtures of these complex themes, there remain many different elements that are distinctly African and ancestral. These common characteristics show, in addition, two particularly important facts: on the one hand, they reveal the wide range of the African musical influence, and on the other hand they show its versatile but expansive potential. The African musical influence has left its mark on much of the New World, from the Caribbean to the Eastern states of the United States in terms of the North, and Brazil and Venezuela to Peru, in terms of the South. More extraordinarily, these various themes still seem to have a strong influence, almost dominance during their mixing with other musical themes.

All authorities on the subject agree that, in the recasting of European musical forms into more typical American themes, major musical factors arise almost always from Negro themes.

Typical American music, in many circumstances, proves to be an African-American hybrid, fruitful and longstanding, which is manifested not only in popular forms, such as *Samba* and Brazilian *Conga*, Haitian meringue, beguine of Martinique, Cuban *Son*, *Jazz*, *Blues* and the North American

Foxtrot, but also in the form of a new classical music like the *Choros*, compositions of Villa-Lobos, the *Batuque* of Fernandez, the Liturgy of Negro Pedro Sanjuan, and the popular opera by Gershwin: *Porgy and Bess*.

I acknowledge that the most interesting aspect is the creative movement of popular Negro influence across the Americas. It should be studied and appreciated, not as a subject of academic controversy about antiquity or the search for basic continuity, but rather to determine how the latter have become factors of influence essential and absolutely necessary to creative continuity. This is not just about the music. If we had begun to discuss influential factors behind the development of the fundamental themes of contemporary modern art, we would be led to identify a truly fruitful contribution of the Negro culture. Here, in fact, the debt would expand to include Europe, because that is where the African sculptures became the primary inspiration of a new aesthetic style, Cubism, which, in the hands of Picasso, Cézanne, Modigliani and others, has revitalized and revolutionized the traditional forms of painting and modern sculpture. Developing in Paris at the beginning of this century this cosmopolitan and open-minded influence is too clearly recognized to be detailed here. Despite their own originality, brilliant creations, and contributions, these artists have always been willing to grant more credit to the entire African source of their inspiration. In fact, African sculptures were a vogue that still persists, and such treasures were transported from the dusty cabinets of ethnology museums and art collectors. Certainly the Negro contribution has not always been as significant in other aspects of cultural life. Neither should it be expected. Culture—we realize more and more—is a complex product, to which all nations and races make their contribution, which is all the more important as people become more civilized. All the more reason to acknowledge what has usually been the part and the contribution of the Negro. Another important point, we should, and that includes us Negroes, not study culture, write or teach history, according to the norms of a racial or national egotism. Although the Negro considers this branch of knowledge as a base of legitimate pride and social morality, as a reason to respect his personality, and although he must inevitably use this teaching as a defense, in reply to critics of his race that could deny him any participation in the evolution of human culture, the present generation should, when studying our history and culture, progressively adhere to an objective method and universal design. This is, without exception, the current trend of African Studies, and what motivates the work of new schools and young researchers. By this method of work, we can claim the value of the Negro and also contribute to a congenial understanding between the races. Based on a system of reciprocal exchange that characterizes the American hemisphere, the new data on the interpretation of cultures and social life indeed allow us to go beyond a simple restoration of the past or rehabilitation of our own tradition to lay the foundations of a friendship and cross-cultural collaboration.

When these new studies are publicized cultural democracy will be more securely widespread. Summarizing these new studies on Africa would take more time than we have, and would depend on much more than enough technical detail to interest a lay audience. For the dedicated student who is interested in the details and in the subject documentation, there is, fortunately, a large body of literature available that deals with various aspects of African culture, in relation to its American descent. In this regard, I would recall a few works out of the ordinary, such as *The Negro Soul* and *The Black Africa*, by Maurice Delafosse, Carter Woodson's book: *The African Heritage*, that of Dr. Du Bois: *Black Brothers, Then and Now*, and the recently released Herskovits: *The Myth of the Negro Past*. There is also the significant work by Ortiz: *Afro-Cuban Studies*, definitive studies on *The Negro in Brazil*, by Arthur Ramos and Gilberto Freyre and the more recent, Donald Pierson. In this respect also, it is worth mentioning the work of Anténor Firmin on *The Equality of Human Races*, as a precise study and honest discussion of principles. *The Rehabilitation of the Black Race*, by Hannibal Price, also deserves mention.

What is important for researchers of general interest and especially for us laymen is the radical change in the design of human problems that characterizes the new anthropology, a design which, despite doctrinal differences on specific conclusions, must be regarded as a true synthesis of the best shared scientific opinion. This is a fundamental and revolutionary perspective of great cultural significance. Although they recognize some Negro and African traits as unique and specific, contemporary scientists have abandoned the assumptions and pseudoscientific suppositions, which unfortunately have influenced and dominated the conceptions and perspectives of many authors in the past, and which currently continues in an unfortunate way to influence lay opinion, in particular, the assumption of innate racial characteristics. Wherever such characteristics meet they must be explained in the spirit of the new schools defined by the search for historical causes and specific social, or cultural influences that can be, even when they are not clearly understood, traced using a methodical search and analysis. Thus, we can no longer from the scientific point of view accept these inaccurate, misleading views, and the frequent humiliating interpretations which rely constantly on the principle of the exception of race. Because we know that no explanation of this kind exists outside of the judgment of amateurs, and that they are valid only in the spirit of racist theorists, here, we must condemn the postulates of Negrophile racism as much as Negrophobic racists. None of them serve the cause of truth and ultimately do not contribute to a better understanding of society. Hasty generalizations, whether favorable or not, are far from being in agreement with the scientific method. These two forms of error must be relegated to the past, and we have to substitute for these, interpretations that explain the features and behavior of a racial group by the same factors and influences which, under similar conditions and in similar circumstances, are likely to explain the features and behavior of any other racial group. It is necessary to stop here a moment to remember, for example, that the basis of the analysis reveals today so many developments in the sociology of the Negro peasant, which was laid by Thomas and Znaniecki in their study of the Polish peasant in the United States, and that many of the new concepts that allow anthropology to penetrate the African culture emerge from the considerable groundbreaking work of the great genius of American anthropology, the late Franz Boas. Also significant, are his students and disciples who are among the many leaders of schools of modern anthropology. It is also interesting to note, that in addition to its scientific objectivity, this kind of study of popular habits constitutes a truly human approach and can rightly be considered a claim on democratic values in the area of understanding culture.

Hopefully, this new design will penetrate further into the field of social relations. Moreover, the phenomena of cultural interpenetration go well beyond the simple moral plan. Studied objectively and correctly interpreted, they provide no justification nor any support to conventional notions about culture, with their false interpretation of power, prestige or racial exclusivity. Modern views in fact consider the cultural influence as a double reciprocal process that is not only top down, but also bottom up. If the master has an influence on the slave, the slave in some respects has an influence on the master. Where antagonistic groups are involved their influence still remains reciprocal, the differences that divide them are the differences of race, class, or nationality. Our current knowledge of culture thus results in a well-defined consequence: on the one hand, the scientific repudiation of racist doctrines and of racial superiority, and on the other hand, moral and intellectual support to the democratic conceptions of human society.

Consider now, in the time we have left, some implications of these findings on some of the traditional concepts, both scientific and popular, concerning Africa, African cultures, social history and the influence of various branches of the Negro race in America.

We will begin, if you will allow me, with a fairly lengthy quotation from Herskovitz's "Social History of the Negro." He said:

> On the whole, it is assumed that the African who was imported into the New World came as a "naked savage," with a cultural background which had neither sufficient depth nor enough vitality to stand against the impact of the experiences of slavery. It is further assumed, as a corollary to the preceding concept, that even though these "naked savages" might conceivably have had a strong cultural heritage the practice of separating the slaves belonging to the same tribe, coupled with the fact of the diversity of African languages and their lack of mutual intelligibility, would in any case have made it impossible for these slaves to preserve what they might have brought with them in the way of cultural endowment. Therefore, in considering New World Negroes, the problems that arise from daily contact between Negroes and whites have absorbed the attention of students, and a few attempts have been made to determine whether or not the behavior of this folk exhibits anything that may be referred to African origins. Indeed, the matter has gone further than this; it has been taken for granted by most students, both Negro and white, that the behavior of New World Negroes is essentially European behavior—though, to be sure, of a more or less infantile order. Moreover, the point that the African culture could be sufficiently tenacious so that not only might Africanisms have been retained by Negroes in the New World but that African influences might have infiltrated into certain elements in the behavior of the white population has been regarded as so impossible as to require no verification by students.[1]

However, Herskovits continues,

> Yet it has been demonstrated above how, by a combination of historical and ethnographic methods, it is quite possible to trace New World Negroes to specific points of origin despite the fact that scholarly tradition has had it that these regions from which Negroes were derived might not be recovered except in the most general way. Similarly it has been seen how the Negroes who were brought to the New World, far from being "naked savages," were the carriers of the high cultures of Africa, cultures that, as one student puts

it, display "on the average, a more complex development of government, art, industry, and material culture than the non-literate inhabitants of any other great continental area" (Murdock, 1934, p. xiv).[2] Not only that, but it has been seen how the individuals sold into slavery represented at the least an adequate cross-section of the population, with possibly a weighting to include more than its portion of the upper strata, while, finally, Africanisms have been pointed out again and again in discussing the life of the various New World Negro groups.[3]

To sum up the reasons for such continuity, Herskovits offers this explanation,

The plantation system which was universal in the New World and the conditions of life of the Negro workers were such that large numbers of them were constantly thrown together. Though supervised in their labor, what they did during the evening was of no concern to their masters as long as it did not affect their efficiency and their acquiescence to control. The Negroes on the plantations must, therefore, have lead an inner life of their own, as would seem to be indicated by the fact that among the first specimens deposited in the British Museum was a Gold Coast type of drum, collected in Virginia during the late eighteenth century. It must also be understood that slave children were not ordinarily separated from their mothers, for such cases were sufficiently unusual to give rise to comment. Even when a child was sold away from his mother, he remained in contact with other Negroes whose behavior was not greatly dissimilar from that of his parents. Since the mechanism by means of which tradition is handed down from one generation to the next is the contact of a child with his elders, slave-children thus absorbed and perpetrated the behavior patterns of their parents and associates rather than those of their masters.

Again, the cultural unity of West Africa, which was pointed out in the discussion of African culture areas, is much greater than is commonly conceived. This unity, of course, does not mean that dissimilarities are not present, for they are often sufficiently great to bewilder the student ... In economic life, in fundamental religious beliefs and practices, and in manifestations of the aesthetic, this underlying unity is also apparent. Granting that the slaves could not at first understand each other, this difficulty must have been surmounted when they learned the tongue of their masters sufficiently well to speak the pidgin dialects that arose, and once pidgin was created, it was natural for the unity of West African cultures to become a significant factor in the maintenance and perpetuation of aboriginal patterns.

A third reason for the retention of Africanisms in the New World was the leadership that Africans of the ruling, warrior, and priestly classes continued to exert in their new home. This leadership was principally evident in the numerous revolts which occurred wherever slavery obtained. In the Caribbean and Guianas, in Brazil and in the United States—even on the slave-ships—these revolts went on intermittently, as recounted in contemporary records, and indicated by the increasing severity of the penalties for rebellion that, as time went on, were authorized by the New World makers of law.[4]

"It is obvious," concludes the passage,

that in the New World these African patterns of behavior have exhibited a vitality and a tenaciousness that far transcends the concept ordinarily held concerning their living quality ... Just as it must not be thought that Negro cultures in Africa are in the process of dissolution in the face of European contact, so it must not be held that contact with Europeans in the New World has not enormously modified the African behavior of the Negroes brought here. The point that cannot be emphasized too greatly is that cultural contact is a matter of give and take, and that although Africanisms have persisted in the New World they are to be seen only as a result of extended analysis, while in Africa European expansion and conquest have left their mark on the indigenous civilizations. Similarly, both in Africa and the New World, the degree of interaction between European and African cultures varies with geographical regions and according to the aspect of culture under consideration.[5]

However, the conclusions of Herskovits have been supported by an increasing number of authorities on the subject, as well as by the results of their research.

So what we can reasonably conclude is surely this:

(1) Despite the brutal destruction of the external forms of African culture, the Negro did not arrive in America with nothing. Instead, he brought considerable social and spiritual baggage, a rather favorable legacy of customs and social habits, and more importantly, a strong social tradition and a powerful moral discipline.

(2) It is only on such a basis that we can explain the rapid and fruitful assimilation by the Negro, of White culture and his immediate and perfect understanding of the moral values of Christianity.

(3) Throughout the period of slavery, and despite the demoralization imposed by the concubinage of the regime of slavery, this tradi-

tional loyalty to the ancestral tribal customs and family ties, were eventually attached to White family institutions, which strengthened their feelings. This is generally accepted even by those who do not fully understand these phenomena.

(4) Finally, the actual strength and influence of these elements of aboriginal West African cultures must be observed, not only in the phenomena of fragmentary dispersion of primitive survivals, but again, more clearly, the many factors which, by assimilation, were preferred and accepted in American culture.

The force of the tradition is so strong in our thought that despite the acceptance of these views by several authorities, and despite the many facts they bring in support of it, one should not expect to see these ideas being adopted immediately. It is often easier to believe what is familiar rather than what seems fairer—whether it is a fact or a simple judgment that follows good sense. Many confrontations between judgments and facts not only illustrate popular taste for false interpretation of speculations concerning the Negro, but they will bring a greater light and will show the exactitude of a more scientific method of social interpretation. Let us take, as our first example, the current conception: that is, by comparison with transplanted Africans, American Negroes have started from zero from a cultural point of view. That erroneous supposition, arisen from an arrogant attitude and a kind of condescension confuse the loss by the slave of external forms of his original culture with a supposed complete lack of memory and social discipline. This was not the case at all. I have even heard the following thesis, espoused as a sort of compliment to the Negro: praised for the unprecedented miracle of his progress, considering that for generations he had been submitted to the most odious savagery and in spite of all could be able to master the most learned civilization. If one follows the logic of this thought, this is a compliment that cuts both ways and whose whole value is reduced to a sentimental flattery and emptiness. The objective truth is that no social miracle of this kind has ever been realized from the historical point of view. From the slave ship to the slave hut and the arbitrarily controlled plantations, most of the imported Africans had to shrink back from their previous condition and cultures. A great deal of social capacity and effort were required to reconstitute intimate life, and, without the help of his own culture and discipline, neither relative progress nor assimilation would have been possible. And if someone could doubt the active role of discipline and the memory of African cultures, one would have only to consider the survival nearly intact of constitutional forms and customs in the fugitive slave communities of Jamaica and Cuba; in the same way that the history of an African type of social organization in the slave villages of Brazil, known as the "The Republic of Palmares,"[6] or—a more decisive fact—the manifestations of African culture that one can still observe in the community of "Bush Negroes" of Dutch Surinam and inside Guyana.

It seems clear that we must do justice to the influence of the African past and its cultural heritage, in addition credit must be granted to the cultural contacts of the Negro in colonial America. We must consider also that the pagan past is not invariably the source of a phenomenon of backwardness, this must be admitted necessarily, today as yesterday, in Negro life. Many of these phenomena, instead of being African survivals or atavisms are the result of the negative effects of slavery. Their primary causes are the demoralizing effects of the slavery regime itself and also the consequence of the disadvantages caused by isolation and misery, which still persists and characterizes the Negro "ghetto." All this, in many circumstances explains the setbacks that are frequently attributed to African origins because what were really Negro ancestral cultures were unknown.

Some competent anthropologists believe that during the period of the Atlantic Slave Trade, the main civilizations of West Africa were equal from a cultural viewpoint to the provincial cultures of Middle Age Europe during the crusades. And—it is worth noting—that systematic exchange of embassies and commercial missions have existed between the cultures and the courts of Portugal, Spain and even of France, these same movements thereby promoted the slave trade. Rattray's observations on the Ivory Coast's social and political life, the detailed description of the kingdom of Dahomey by Herskovits, and so many faithful reconstructions of indigenous life in Nigeria before the harmful influence of modern colonial penetration allow us to realize what types of complex and relatively advanced civilizations constituted the background of many slave groupings.

No one would say that these African heritages have had as direct an influence as that of other American groups that have migrated freely. The slave was the least favored of migrants. His original language, religion and customs were taken away from the start. But the indirect influence of his culture was no less important, and ancestral factors when they were strong enough to reappear long after being dominated by others were sufficiently powerful to influence primary social habits. So brutal was the slave's existence, that psychological reactions had a lot to do with slave life and they have in fact determined the course of all social history of the Negro. The indigenous in the Caribbean and elsewhere have always systematically been submitted to the slavery regime but the incompatibility of his customs and his passive resistance despite the use of force made his use as laborer impossible. The cultural past of the Negro made possible not only his incorporation into the plantation economy, but facilitated his rapid and effective assimilation of White culture.

With the best scientific rigor, we should invoke the Negro original type of society to explain his behavior. He was not nomadic, but for many generations he has been accustomed to an organized, stable and complex society. Shortly after his arrival in America, we find him ultimately employed and initially linked to the plantation life; in the colonial family Negro women were employed as caregivers to children, housewives, and pets. Does not this phenomenon have something to do with the African past and with the fundamentally patriarchal institutions that constituted West Africa, the clan—as with many social formations that resemble the American plantation system of concubinage? It is absurd to think that coming from an organized society on a communal and cooperative basis, the Negro has learned to develop cooperative systems exclusively under the master's whip. The evidence of it is that the custom was typical not only toward the master, but toward one another in the slaves' native societies. One can reasonably believe that a good part of his obedience and loyalty, if often praised, derives initially from the previous experience of tribal life and not from the master's authority and presence to which he would have been faithful "like a domestic animal." A big part of the traditional patience of the slave and much of his fatalistic resignation come also from his long experience as a man of the tropics in whom nature itself has incorporated such attitudes. We should remind ourselves that the model, once installed by the first arrivals, tended to perpetuate itself by tradition, at the same time that it was constantly reinforced by successive series of African importations.

Everything that has just been said indicates sufficiently how the typical Negro attitudes and reactions should be interpreted, and all of that differs singularly from the conventional manner of doing so. It is contrary to the facts to consider the Negro as an undisciplined, amoral, and savage being incapable of cooperation, who was brought to these shores with nothing other than his docile charms, his superstitious ignorance, but who was afterwards tamed by slavery and civilized by Christianity. In his work entitled *Voyage au Congo* (*Voyage to the Congo*), André Gide tells a marvelous story that brings us some light on these facts. He said having seen litigants walk along side by side to the point of reaching their court, sleeping together, eating together, assisting themselves mutually and repeating together the return trip after the judge's decision had been known,—and in the same way announcing publically to the village chief the sentence and the sanction. The ones who know Africa well know how this fact is characteristic of life on this continent.

Indeed, we find that it is impossible to consider Negroes as a grouping that would have developed its culture in America without giving anything back, or as a group that would have given all its vitality to the civilization of its masters and would not have, somehow been accountable for the weaknesses of his own culture. We cannot suppose that the first contacts of Africans with advanced moral ideas came from his conversion to Christianity, especially since Christianity has had no real meaning for him. If the Negro could so rapidly assimilate Christianity it is because he had in his moral customs and beliefs similar elements to those of Christianity. This is the most probable considering that religion was taught to a group of illiterate slaves, and generally by preachers that were themselves by and large semi-illiterate. Add to this that many communities were not at all enthusiastic about the idea of teaching Christianity to the slaves until they discovered the exemplary spirit of sacrifice with which slaves could interpret religion.

The content of the Spirituals demonstrates the extraordinary assimilation of the teachings of Christianity into the spirit and heart of the Negro peasant. The Negro's deep spirituality exceeded the scope of the teachings that were given to him and without manifesting any allusion to dogma or theology, several of Christianity's fundamental concepts and particularly its social teaching were already familiar to the Africans. Most of the pagan religions possessed very advanced moral concepts on supernatural origin and life control, individual and collective sin, moral and social values, benefit of virtues, ancestral immortality, obligation of fraternity, goodness and mutual assistance. Smart missionaries finally admitted, as shown by the conclusions of the *Le Zoute* Conference in Belgium, which affirmed the necessity for the missionary to use the codes and the systems of indigenous teaching as the basis of moral education in indigenous life without developing the old antagonism between ancestral religion and the new religion.[7] Though it is too late to repair the great injustices that result from the mistakes and difficulties of the past, we find in them the grounds for a better attitude in the future. This new attitude results from a more judicious study of African cultures and the new horizons that they engendered. There is certainly little interest for us to explain the religious life of the American Negro by assuming as before a particular and mysterious racial religiosity. The two principal factors are, more exactly, the deep need of religion that is manifested in the Negro as a sort of consolation for the sad conditions of slavery and the deep moral character of his ancestral tradition and teaching.

Thus, the time has arrived where the traits of African groupings and racial characters of the Negro must be considered on the same basis as those of other groupings and races. We must explain them as for instance we will explain the mystical trait of the Hindu and the characteristic hospitality of the Muslim, the characteristic reserve of the English, or the pragmatic trait of Americans. We know that all of them come from a series of historical adaptations that are cultivated and survive as real social traditions. Although they are relatively stable or typical, all of these features have some exceptions within each group, and they are modifiable through education or protracted changes of the environment. In addition, these traits, when they are scientifically explained are not the source of any conflict of interpretation as the contradictory fairy tales which sometimes underlie the loyalty and sometimes the lack of responsibility of the Negro, and in fact vary according to the mood of the person who developed them and seeks to impose his point of view. The characteristics must be described according to a fair historical perspective: those that are good and those that seem bad should be attributed objectively to their real causes. If for instance, the discipline of "the frontier" and later the machine are considered primarily responsible for the American practical inclination, the social history of being overworked and implied lack of initiative involved in working under slavery, can, with equal legitimacy explain the apathy and what one wants well to call "the laziness" of the Negro. Some resemblances in past cultural and social experiences have effectively forged the common denominators that characterize the Negro, but the differences, are determined by the cultural contacts that also explain once and for all the evident disparities that make a Haitian Negro French, a Brazilian Negro Portuguese, a Venezuelan Negro Spanish, a United States Negro Nordic Northern (American) from a cultural point of view. Instead of opposing the sentimental objections to what might characterize Negro groups, Negro intellectuals have at their disposal an intelligent alternative that constitutes at the same time the only really scientific attitude: work to investigate and explain the causes of these characteristics. Because all of these traits can be explained and understood in regard to the experience that has created them, we can substitute true and enlightened interpretations for superficial or caricatured considerations that for too long have been accepted to explain Negro racial traits and African cultural characteristics.

This results in many practical applications that it is good to signal briefly here. In the first place, after Guyana, Haiti remains the most important center of African survivals in the Americas. As such, it constitutes a precious laboratory for the study of vestiges that disappear so rapidly and remain essential not only for the historical study of the evolution of our race but also for that of human culture itself. Scholarly Haitian men have been very interested in these problems and their contributions on this topic are rather consistent. However, few things have been done in terms of comparative studies capable of linking together local studies with the mass of available materials on Afro-Brazilian, Afro-Cuban, Afro-American and African studies in general. This will have to be the next step and it should be possible for us to discover enough of the suggestive facts that have nevertheless remained unknown.

With the study of the influence of French factors, the study of Haitian ethnology and folklore can gain a lot by being affiliated with other African sources, particularly the works of *L'Ecole des Sciences Sociales* (The School of Social Sciences) of Sao Paulo, of *Societes d'Etudes Afro-Cubans* (Afro-Cuban Study Societies) of Havana, of *l'Institut International de Langues et de Cultures Africaines* (International Institute of African Languages and Cultures) of London and many Societies of the United States, especially The Association for the Study of Negro Life and History whose founder Dr. Carter Woodson has been the director for twenty years. It is with a certain satisfaction that we notice the increasing interest that is developing in Haiti for these studies and we hope in an optimistic way to see Haitian works begin to radiate abroad, while Haiti contributes so much to African studies.

To finish, we would like to say, what African studies can bring to the contemporary world. For this is not as was said before, a purely academic matter. The current war leads Africa into the orbit of World civilization after the long and sad eclipse that constitutes the colonial phase of its History. Certain practical reasons will lead African colonial regimes to an unavoidable recasting that will benefit not only Africa but the stability of a durable world peace. Colonial imperialism, which in Africa has been a permanent source of rivalries and international struggles, should be transformed into a basis of international agreement and lead to a just and constructive cooperation upon satisfactory political and economic programs. Africa will thus become an experimental land for a new internationalism.

Two reforms are unavoidably included within this program: one is the reorganization of colonial politics according to democratic views that especially take into consideration the happiness and development of indigenous peoples, and the other will be the development of such politics according to an intelligent program based on meticulous internal needs and potentialities of African life and its indigenous cultures. As Western culture and African culture meet more and more, not ever to be separated, we need a sound concept for the fusion of what these two elements offer as better in order to replace this incompatible mixture of water and oil and this mimetic re-Europeanization that predominates in Africa today. Thus the practical aspects of contemporary African studies can alone, thanks to scientific support, guide a task as considerable as that of cultural reform and integration.

For several reasons that are far from sentimental and stem only from democratic theory, the participation of the cultivated African to the realization of such a program seems absolutely imperative. The program would simply be neither realizable nor efficient without his participation. And for pragmatic reasons I would add that it would be wise and necessary to allow New World Negroes to participate in it in an active way. Without having formal colonial objectives, American nations have great interest in participating in the democratic and progressive reorganization of Africa. And it seems also to me that they have historical moral obligations for having been beneficiaries for many generations of the Slave Trade and its incommensurable contributions to the New World economic development. Fortunately too, the American hemisphere can offer within this great humanitarian enterprise of the future the constructive lesson of fertile assimilation by the American Negro into modern forms of civilization and culture, despite the disadvantages they have presented him with so far. This fortunate assimilation certainly put the American Negro into the position of becoming the logical and strategic intermediary of educational reconciliation between Africa and the modern Western world. And if the professions of faith in democracy are sincere, a representative part of the fifty or sixty millions of African descent in American will not be refused the occasion to participate in the service of a constructive social order. They can prepare themselves for it under the condition that this task is undertaken on an international basis with the larger participation of all of those who would have a contribution to make. In these revolutionary days, this idea is neither an excessive hope, nor impossibility. Here, only our lack of interest or specialized knowledge stands between us, and what we can envisage as one of the greatest opportunities offered to us.

These new horizons we will say to conclude, we discover in the new knowledge of Africa and African things. Such studies promise:

(1) to give the Negro an accurate knowledge of himself and his own historical past, thus contributing to the development of a collective morality and respect for the Negro personality.

(2) to provide an objective scientific basis for the accurate interpretation of racial traits and the interaction of Negro elements with other cultures, thus providing the basis for a better understanding of the American hemisphere's social and cultural history.

(3) To finally provide the fairest interpretations on African cultures and to lay down in a scientific way the basis of a revisionary program of colonial politics, and thus working to a reconstruction of the basis of continental African life.

NOTES

1. Herskovits, Melville J. "Social History of the Negro." In *A Handbook of Social Psychology: Volume 1*, edited by Carl Murchison, 207–67. New York: Russell and Russell, 1935. 255–256.

2. Murdock, G. P. *Our Primitive Contemporaries*. Oxford, England: Macmillan, 1934.

3. Herskovits, "Social History of the Negro," 256.

4. Herskovits, "Social History of the Negro," 258–259.

5. Herskovits, "Social History of the Negro," 259–260.

6. Starting in 1600, a colony of maroons is actually established in the Brazilian northeast, with the complicity of the indigenous peoples, and resisted for nearly a century military assaults by the Dutch and Portuguese.

7. International Missionary Council was been founded in 1921 with the aim of developing cooperation between missionary societies in Africa; it held several international lectures, of which, that of Zoute in 1926 on the missionary work. Its archives are saved in London in the Library of the School of Oriental and African Studies.

Lecture 3: The Negro's Position in North American Culture

Our task in the next three lectures is to describe as carefully and objectively as possible the position of the Negro in the United States of America. It is not so easy a task in so short a compass. There is also another difficulty. As a human situation, unlike a physical one for which we can arrive at a precise solution, it is subject to several interpretations. And so, in offering to you what are, of course, my own most considered and conscientious opinions, I must warn you nevertheless that they are personal after all, and that no one man's opinion can be taken as the whole truth about a situation so complex or on which there are of necessity so many schools of thought. Indeed I hope that in due course of time you will have opportunity to hear other American scholars from the United States state their version and interpretation of the complex and fascinating social situation of the American Negro.

In today's lecture, I shall attempt to give an overall picture of the Negro's cultural position in our North American setting. This naturally will deal with the activities and contributions of the intellectual classes,— the elite, although not without some consideration of the important factor of the folk culture. In the lecture to follow, we shall try to obtain an overall view of the Negro's sociological position, which will focus on the condition and problems of the masses of this largest and oldest of the North American minorities. Here we shall be interested in social trends as well as social prospects, since, I take it; your main interest is not primarily in history but in the contemporary situation as it confronts us today.

© The Editor(s) (if applicable) and The Author(s) 2016   41
J.A. Carter, *African American Contributions to the Americas'*
Cultures, DOI 10.1057/978-1-137-56572-3_4

Finally in the third, we shall try to give you some more concrete notion of Negro achievement, using as representative of our racial progress, thumbnail sketches of certain significant careers in the various fields of human endeavor–art, literature (*belles lettres*), science, education, political leadership, labor organization, social reform, women's progress, technical and applied science.

As with a considerable sense of familiarity I turn toward what for me is the home front of race, I am aware that I am directing your attention to what is away from home and, unfamiliar. One or two basic points of orientation must, therefore, be given. One is that the situation, for from being stationary, is changing even as we discuss it, all the more so because of the rapid developments of war conditions which for us, on the whole as a racial minority have been inducing rapid change and in a favorable direction. Indeed, with such social situations and problems what often matters most is not where they are at a given moment as in which direction they are moving and at what rate of change. The other is to avoid that general error we are all apt to make of stereotyping our mental picture of a national situation, just as we color a country symbolically on the map. The only adequate scientific picture, especially of the racial situation in North America would correspond to one of the more scientific kinds of re-presentation, like the elevation maps, that would show specifically the regional and other variations that actually exist. Both because of its colossal almost continental size and the wide variation of its social cultures and traditions, the system of race relations in the United States varies so widely that if we accepted one type of situation as the national norm, it would be entirely misleading. In the next lecture, which is more definitely sociological in approach, we will see how radically different in their pattern of race relations several of these varying regions are, and that this variation is far more complex than the old historical difference between the northern and the southern states. We shall discover, for example, that in some states or provinces what we call the Negro problem is relatively non-existent or that in passing, say, from the Mid-West to the far west region of from there again into the great Southwest, one must pass, so to speak from one social climate to another quite characteristically different. In short, it is not safe to generalize on too grand a scale concerning this racial problem.

But there exists an even more important dimension of variation than the regional one. It is ideological, and is responsible for the peculiar status of the race question in the United States. It arises from the fact that throughout our national history, and particularly for the century and a quarter since the dawn of the anti-slavery movement, North American public opinion has been sharply divided itself on the race issue. To realize this clearly we have only to call to mind the symbolic fact of four long years of Civil War, 1860–1865, fought over the issue of the slave system and the emancipation of the Negro. Even at the time the division of the national mind and conscience was not wholly regional between the South and the North. There were, as we may learn from the close study of the historical record, antislavery factions in the South, though of course in the minority, and proslavery factions in the North. This general division of public opinion, still existing today and tending more and more to divorce itself from regional traditions and geographical boundaries is, in my opinion, the most characteristic and hopeful fact of our national situation about race.

Why? Because it means, as indeed it has meant all along historically, that the struggle for Negro rights, though it relates to a racial condition and situation, is nevertheless not merely a racial issue but an interracial cause and movement. The abolition movement with its notable participation of the intellectual and moral elite of the white race, set a biracial pattern for public agitation and social reform which with few exceptions has been followed ever since. Occasionally we have by way of exception an all-Negro movement such as the Garvey movement, but the typical alignment is that of liberal elements of both races allying to crusade against reactionary forces and opinion. The National Association for the Advancement of Colored People, the National Urban League, the Southern Congress for Human Welfare, with bi-racial membership and organization, which was formed in the Southern United States to work for reform of Southern reactionary practices. This example is enough to explain why the issue of race has remained so important, being both a national issue and the subject of public discussion. It shows at the same time why this problem has occupied such a prominent place in our political life, and occupies an important position either of imagination or controversy, in its manifestations in our literature. There remains and will remain for a long time, a national issue of exceptional importance, and of considerable gravity.

Another interesting fact, culturally, is the intimate association between the moral and intellectual elite of the white majority and elite leaders of the Negro minority. This association with only an occasional decade or so of lapse of crusading interest, ever since those noble days of the anti-slavery movement, when Wendell Phillips, Charles Sumner, Henry Ward Beecher, Wm. Lloyd Garrison, Harriet Beecher Stowe and eventually Abraham Lincoln, became veritable champions of Negro rights. History alone can reliably select the immortals of this our own generation, but the mention merely of such a symbolic few as Madame Roosevelt, Pearl Buck, Frantz Boas, Julius Rosenwald, Frank Graham of the University of North Carolina, Bishop McConnell, Father La Farge, Rabbi Wise, will indicate what one means by claiming that this liberal alliance is as much in force today as then. Needless to say, such alignments are the pivots of present progress, which as I have already indicated seems to be rapidly increasing its momentum.

One of the outstanding effects of this generation-old crusade for freedom and larger opportunity was the stimulation of unusual cultural effort and unusual cultural achievement among Negros in many instances. The incentives, you see, were not just personal ambition but a group cause, and the objective was not the limited one of attracting racial attention but to catch the nation's, even in some cases, the international ear. The anti-slavery struggle, therefore, early evoked considerable Negro talent and brought it forward rapidly to articulate and matured expression. As early as 1773, Phyllis Wheatley, a talented little slave girl in Boston, was writing Odes to Freedom, a year or so later to address a dedication Ode to General Washington on Taking Command of the Continental Armies, which, to the credit of the man who was to become the first President of the United States, was duly and gratefully acknowledged. In 1799, another Negro, in New England of course, then the center of American liberalism, wrote under the pseudonym of "Othello," a prose arraignment of slavery as inconsistent with both Christianity and democracy. From this point on an increasing number of Negro figures, often fugitive slaves joined in effectively in the abolitionist movement, imitating creditability and some of them rivaling their white Abolitionist friends and associates. The middle of the period, 1831–1839 produced such figures as Martin Delany, McCune Smith, Ringgold Ward, Wm. Wells Brown, Thomas Redmond, Henry Highland Garnett, orators and writers whose works will stand critical comparison of their models,–Garrison, Gerritt Smith, Beecher, Sumner and Wendell Phillips, and who, as we know, shared the public platform abroad as well as in America with the outstanding authors of their day in the campaign against slavery. This was, indeed, a great accomplishment for a generation of freed men, most of whom learned their letters after their escape from slavery, but whom, within ten or fifteen years, were campaigning on the public platforms of New England, the Middle States, London, Belfast, Edinburgh, London, Paris.

An interesting sidelight on the closeness of the collaboration during this period is the fact that the fugitive slave story of Josiah Henson, later published, was taken orally by Harriet Beecher Stowe as the basic plot and characterization plan of *Uncle Tom's Cabin*.

The symbolic figure of this period was Frederick Douglass, whom Haitians remember as one of the greatest of the American Ministers to Haiti, but who for us was not only the great hero of the Abolitionist and Civil War periods but also of early Reconstruction. From a feeble beginning of the Narrative of His Escape from Slavery in 1945, Douglass rose to national and international fame as an orator, newspaper edition publicist: he was the outstanding spokesman of the Equal Rights school of thought over a span of nearly fifty years. You will be told that Booker Washington is the symbolic American Negro: he was a great figure and made a significant contribution which will be discussed in the next lecture. But it is Frederick Douglas who more and more looms as the race here, especially in the minds of the contemporary younger generation, and precisely for his uncompromising advocacy of equal rights and interracial collaboration on the same democratic premise of equal opportunity and full unhampered participation. It is interesting to note that the compromise solutions of the Booker Washington school of thought, not having been any too successful in practice, are today losing their hold on representative Negro thought. And to a degree also in the social philosophy of the closest friends of the Negro cause. As they do, it is the figure and position of Douglass that looms up, with modernized reinforcements of course, to take its place.

But for the moment we must concern ourselves more particularly with literary and cultural developments. After the enthusiasm of the North had spent itself in the furious and bitter campaign of anti-slavery and the early Reconstruction enactment of Civil Rights, there was a period of considerable reaction and decline. In this moral lull, Southern writers and publicists began that remarkable campaign of self-justification which set out to glorify the lost Southern Cause and romanticize the ancient slave regime. For a considerable while the subtle and entertaining writings of white Southern novelists as Thomas Nelson Page and George Cable dominated the public's interest. This school of thought created the stereotypes by which the Negro is still popularly known in America, and only with the greatest difficulty can these half-truths be displaced by subsequent scientific and literary work that studies more closely and truthfully the actualities of Negro life and character and the true historical facts about the slave regime. Even Joel Chandler Harris, to whom the world owes Uncle Ramus and the salvaging of an important segment of Negro folklore, fell somewhat into the pitfalls of this false sentimental glorification of the Old South and slavery, with all its clichés of happy, well-treated retainers, contented serfs and carefree, happy-go-lucky pickaninies. This was, we know, one side of plantation life: the more modern realistic writers of our own generation have clearly shown us another, more somber and socially not so patriarchal, humane and innocent. The one outstanding Negro novelist of this period, Charles Chestnutt, tried in vain by more carefully documented fiction, to gainsay this Cable-Page influence. The public would not believe his realism, until convinced twenty years later by our contemporary Southern—Glascow, Faulkner, Caldwell and others who unanimously substantiate Chestnutt and belie Cable, Harris, Page and Co.

In contrast to Chestnutt, our most considerable Negro poet of the nineties was immediately acclaimed by the general public, partly because he was a considerably gifted poet, but also because his dialect portrayals of the Negro peasant coincided with the popular vogue and idea of what was racially most typical. At best his work in this vein can be said to represent not the modern but the vanishing Negro, the race at a certain stage of its history and a certain limited picture even at that. An authoritative critic has said: Dunbar was the articulate end of the regime, and not the first of modern Negro poets. He himself rebelled against the popular overemphasis on his dialect poetry, and was more proud of his more representative personal lyric poetry in legitimate English and his more serious short stories and novels. But he will always be known more as the dialect poet of "When Malindy Sings" and "When the Corn Pone's Hot" than as the author of the "Ode to Ethiopia," the sonnets to Robert Gould Shaw, Frederick Douglass and Booker Washington or his serious novel *Sport of the God's*.

Just about this time (1895–1905) there came about another important stage in the cultural development of Negro life. A tragic but inevitable split developed between the cause of the masses and the cause of the elite. The pressure of majority prejudice, forcing the advance guard of the rapidly increasing "talented tenth" back on the masses,–that pattern of wholesale, undifferentiating racial discrimination so different from the Latin-American class pattern of distinctions, was mainly responsible for this embittered reaction. But so also was an internal feud over race programs and objectives. The cause of the masses found its protagonist in Booker Washington, and in his program of industrial education, political compromise and cultural *laissez-faire*. His autobiography *Up From Slavery*, since became an American classic, made this wing of Negro thought articulate.

The opposition faction crystallized around another notable book. *The Souls of Black Folk*, that was written by one of our leading intellectuals, Dr. W. E. B. Du Bois. This book articulated the opposite cause of equal civic rights, undifferentiated education, repudiation of any acceptance of a bi-racial compromise. Against great initial odds of wide majority support for the Washington formulas, the equal rights camp finally succeeded in developing equal rights organizations and the support of white and Negro liberals. Finally a decade later it won over the posts and men of letters, only at the cost of much bitter controversy and of a somewhat dull interim of propagandist rather than creative writing. The *Souls of Black Folk*, ideologically vindicated became a recognized classic, but only after the American public began to realize that in gaining in Dr. Du Bois's preoccupations with these social movements an effective race publicist they had probably lost one of the generation's most gifted literary talents.

This period of assertion and protest did perform a valuable service, however. It prepared the way for the ascendancy of the Negro intellectual in scholarship, art and letters. Instead of the orator and publicist, the poet and artist and thinker came to the fore. From 1912 to 1915 on, with some temporary interruptions but also some unusual motivations from the first World War, Negro culture went on to a wholly new stage and scope of development. One career must be mentioned in passing as spanning both sides of this transition, that of the late James Weldon Johnson, who began as a disciple and imitator of Dunbar's to end his career much later as one of the pioneers of the new racialist expression that was later named the school of the "New Negro."

Immediately preceding this, however, came a school of social protest generated in part by the ironies of the war "to make the world safe for democracy" when these younger Negro poets and writers faced the realization that as yet the Negro American lacked the benefits of full democracy. In reaction against outside appeals and didactic humanitarian rhetoric these younger poets turned to the racial audience, proposing assertive self-reliance. It was largely emotional radicalism, born of the minority situation, but naturally some phases of it found congenial refuge in the political radicalism of the times. Fenton Johnson, Rosco Jameison, Langston Hughes in his earlier poems and Claude McKay were of this group, the latter being, interestingly enough, an adopted North American of Jamaican birth. Fenton Johnson's "I'm tired of building up somebody else's civilization" was a keynote reaction. Bitter as was this cynical disillusionment, it was the tonic necessary for the recovery of racial self-respect and confidence of a new generation.

Fortunately at this very juncture and reassuring forces were moving in the general world of American art and letters. White liberalism was redis-covering the Negro and beginning to take a serious interest in Negro life and materials. This was not the old philanthropic interest in the Negro,— or it would have been rebuffed by these younger Negro intellectuals: it was, instead, a genuine attempt to reinterpret Negro life as bringing a newly discovered source of native materials for American art. In painting, drama and fiction, the new American realism was working toward this general objective, and found Negro subject-matter singularly useful and appropriate. The work of such artists as Stribling Shands, Clement Wood, Ellen Glasgow, Julia Peterkin, Du Bose Heyward in the field of the novel and short story, of Riggley Torrence, Eugene O'Neill, Paul Green and later Heyward, also, in drama and of Winslow Homer, Thomas Eakins, Robert Henri, George Luks in painting led to this new revelation of val-ues and new cultural vogue of serious interest in the Negro artistically. The concurrent development of a strongly racialist school of Negro poets and artists was particularly opportune, and soon the natural alliance was brought about which explains the present favorable cultural entente which I have already described in general outline in my first lecture, and which from about 1920 on has considerably enhanced the Negro's cultural posi-tion and outlook.

Of course, social factors also played a role in this development. There was the basic uplift of increased education and wider economic prosperity. There was, additionally, the important effect of rapid urbanization, as more Negroes moved from the farms to cities and from the South generally. War industry alone is estimated as having shifted over a million and a half Negroes northward between 1917 and 1925. There were the galvanizing shocks of the First World War itself. Finally there was a general resurgence of race-consciousness and group pride, in this setting and generation, positively toned. The new spirit had developed considerable momentum, especially in progressive Negro groups in centers like New York City, Chicago and Washington. Incidentally, the movement could easily have become known as the Harlem movement because Harlem, the largest residential area of the Negro population there, became not only the first organized center of this new school of thought and artistic expression but also was the favored meeting-ground of the white and Negro art-ists, reformers and intellectuals. However, it fell to my good fortune to have been able in 1925 to christen it the "New Negro" movement and to compare it, somewhat presumptively at that time, with cultural revivals like the Irish Renaissance of the previous decade calling it also "the Negro Renaissance." Subsequent developments seem to have justified the faith of the presumption. For almost in geometrical progression since 1925 American Negro cultural expression in scholarship and in the creative arts. The years of the economic depression, 1930 on, saw almost no diminution in these spiritual gains, especially because the various Federal Aid Projects in the fields of fine art, music, the theater, literature writing were to their great credit, be it said, administered almost without any racial discrimination, so that the youngest generation of our creative talent got much needed support and encouragement. In this way there came about the general acceptance of the Negro as a contributor to national culture and as a collaborator in national self-expression.

From the side of the white artist came in this first decade of the movement such epoch-making contributions as O'Niell's *The Emperor Jones*, which in addition to its own influence, reintroduced the Negro actor after a long lapse to the serious Broadway stage. Paul Green's Pulitzer Prize play, *In Abraham's Bosom*, Du Bose Heyward's folk novel *Porgy*, Torrence's inauguration of a Negro Theater in his *Three Plays for a Negro Theater*. From the Negro side came considerable new talent in poetry, drama, fiction and critical *belles lettres*, barely to mention a much augmented output of historical and sociological scholarship. This, too, was the decade that saw the phenomenal success of such Negro singers as and musicians as Harry Burleigh, Roland Hayes, Paul Robeson, Marian Anderson, and trailing that stage of development the debut of the serious Negro composer in figures like Wm. Dawson, Wm. Grant Still, Duke Ellington, who though a Jazz musician, rates as an influential and significant contemporary American composer. Four Negro poets appeared, Claude McKay, Jean Toomer, Countee Cullen, and Langston Hughes, who with James Weldon Johnson, must certainly be reckoned not merely as Negro poets but in any fair survey of leading contemporary American poetry. Their poetry is racial, on the whole, but in a new way. Charles Johnson, now a sociologist but at the time editor of *Opportunity*, one of the leading journals of this movement, has aptly put the difference in these words:—"The new racial poetry of the Negro marks the birth of a new racial consciousness, and the recognition of difference without the usual implications of disparity. It lacks apology, self-pity or the wearying appeals to pity, and the conscious philosophy of defense. In being itself it reveals its greatest charm. In accepting its own life naturally it invests it with new meaning."[1]

Perhaps you will permit the interlude of English quotation to taste the sample flavor of some of this. I quote first Langston Hughes': very well-known, "The Negro Speaks of Rivers," with its reverent and stimulating, but terse panorama of the Negro's racial past:—

> I've known rivers:
> Ancient, dusky rivers.
>
> My soul has grown deep like the rivers.[2]

And again, for both its beautiful transcription of the rhythm of Negro song and speech to poetry, as well as for its sophisticated but reverent reaction to the American Negro past, I quote from Jean Toomer's "Song of the Son" an elegant stanza:

> Pour O pour that parting soul in song,
>
> An everlasting song, a singing tree,
> Caroling softly souls of slavery,
> What they were, and what they are to me,
> Caroling softly souls of slavery.[3]

One can easily see with what an enthusiastic cult of idealistic racialism the Negro Renaissance started. Over romantic as it later turned out to be under the soberer light of problem drama, realistic regional fiction, scholarly and factual sociology, it nevertheless did give this phase of our cultural development a vibrant start and a new and much needed group dynamic. By means of it maturity came into the Negro's formal expression in the arts. The breadth of the cultural stream increased with its depth, for our traditional proficiency in music, poetry, and oratory soon was supplemented by a notably increased productivity in drama, fiction, *belles lettres* and critical scholarship, painting and sculpture. Another marked feature of this period was a deliberate revival of interest in the folk materials, and an attempt not merely to collect and preserve them as folklore, but to use them creatively for new forms of art, especially in drama, formal music and ballet. 1934 saw the production of Wm. Dawson's symphony on Folk Themes the next year Grant Still's Afro-American Symphony, Broadway was startled and captivated a year or so later by Asadata Horton's African ballet, Klunker. You will recall Katherine Dunham's research visit to Haiti: her balletized folk dances based on Negro folk idioms have been among the successes of the last few seasons, just as was indeed the success of the reciprocal visit of Lina Fussman-Mathon's Haitian Dance Troupe under the patronage of your President Lescot. Pride of race led to increased understanding and appreciation of the folk and eventually to that even more distant pride of African ancestry. It is significant to note that, independently about the same time or a little later a similar reaction was taking place in Haitian letters with your group of the Poesie Haitienne Indigene, with the work of Laleau, Roumer, Roumain, Viuex, etc. To put it in the words of one of our best poets, Countee Cullen,

> Lord, I will live persuaded by my own,
> My spirit has come home, that sailed *the doubtful seas.*[4]

In the field of our national music, the influence is of course obvious, America, already under the sway of ragtime since 1912, experienced from 1922 on the jazz age. For twenty years now, in spite of repeated try-outs of new musical contenders, whose average vogue has not lasted two seasons, Negro jazz has dominated popular song and dance, and through it a large part of the emotional and recreational life of the entire country. One might add, the world, considering the world dispersion of jazz in its many varieties, not always, it is to be regretted, are the best varieties exported. The basic source of jazz is the "Blues," a secular form of Negro folk music, second in importance only to the Spirituals. We must never forget that the Blues are a form of folk poetry and ballad expression as well a distinctive musical form, and that many of our poets, black and white, including the outstanding Negro poets Langston Hughes and Sterling Brown, use the themes and idioms of the blues as the base of their poetry. Our veteran musician, Wm. C. Handy, is responsible for their musical vogue. He is credited with "commencing a revolution in the popular tunes of this land comparable only to that brought about by the introduction of ragtime."[5] But it is more to our purpose to call to your attention that fact that jazz music has reached the stage of profoundly influencing serious creative music. First, the unique playing techniques of the Negro jazz musicians have changed the playing possibilities of the wind and the brass and the percussion instruments, and started one of the most lucrative of modern musical professions, the jazz player and virtuoso.

Then, the blues harmonies and subsequent elaborations of them and their rhythms have helped revolutionize modern musical harmony. Jazz music has reached a level of serious cultivation and analysis unprecedented for any previous from of popular music, and in classical jazz the great talents of Negro composers like Ellington, Dett, Fletcher Henderson, Still, Reginald Forsythe have been matched by such serious white jazz composers as Gershwin, Grofe, Greunberg, Aaron Copland, Cesana, Lamar Stringfield and Norton Gould. To this American influence must be added that of jazz upon European composers of the structure of Ernst Krenek, Kurt Weill, Darius Milhaud and Stravinsky. In music, too, the closest of all collaborations to date has occurred; frequently the jazz arranger of the leading white jazz bands is a Negro jazz composer, and the affiliation of white and Negro musicians in this field is notably close and cordial. Thus, our racial music has proved itself creatively potent at all the levels, folk, popular and classical, well fulfilling that prophecy of its determining role in our national music pronounced in 1895 by Dvorak, when he wrote and justified his sponsorship of Negro musical themes in his "New World Symphony."

In the fine arts recent years have seen noteworthy progress. Fifteen years ago there were only one or two painters and sculptors of general note, like Henry O. Tanner, Meta Warrick, May Howard Jackson. Now, thanks to the influence of the new Negro movement, the Harmon Foundation and also the Federal Arts Projects, centers like New York, Philadelphia, Atlanta, and Chicago can muster from a score or so of younger artists creditable work in all the various media. Sculpture, as one might expect, is a strong and original development, in which one must mention particularly our most productive and outstanding representative, Richmond Barthe, a native of New Orleans, but now in New York. He along with Sargent Johnson, Augusta Savage, Wm. Artis and others maintain that ancestral tradition of originality of expression in the plastic arts. As to painters, they are too many to mention. One can only generalize by saying that as their interest in the artistic interpretation of Negro types and Negro life has increased, so too has their technique and mastery of creative individualized expression. As a consequence, their work is rapidly breaking through to general recognition. It is now welcomed in the best galleries, museum collections and annual exhibitions, and not, of course, as Negro but as representative contemporary American art. You have heard, I hope, of Jacob Lawrence, the young Negro painter, who as a lad of nineteen did that modernistic serious of 41 scenes from the life of Toussaint L'Ouverture from his own inspiration and library research in Harlem. He has since risen to maturity and fame through four subsequent series of symbolic tempera panels on the themes respectively of Harriet Tubman, the Negro abolitionist, Frederick Douglass, John Brown and the War Migration of the Negro Northward. The latter series, exhibited in New York a year ago, was one of the art season's sensations: its sale provoked a deadlock of several weeks bargaining, solved eventually by dividing the series between The Museum of Modern Art and The Phillips Memorial Gallery of Washington.

In drama, we still await full maturity of artistic development. Substantial gains, however, have been made. After Torrence and O'Neill, the plays of Paul Green and DuBose Hayward have continued to give increased depth and seriousness to the dramatic portrayal of Negro life and character. A number of the successful plays of the Federal Theater were of Negro subject-matter, among them a predecessor to the recent drama of Selden Rodman, by William DuBois called *Haiti*. It treated the same background of the Haitian Revolution, vividly and with reasonably close historical accuracy,—on the whole, a play worth calling to your attention not only as a past tribute but as meriting, perhaps, re-staging. The outstanding Negro actor, after Paul Robeson and the lamented Rose McClendon, Canada Lee was the Dessalines of this play. Broadway already knew him for a notable performance in what is still the outstanding Negro problem play,—*Stevedore*, a story of the Negro struggle for labor rights and organization, and has again most recently acclaimed his great talent for his performance of the title role of the drama version of Richard Wrights' significant novel,— *Native Son*. These gains in dignified and unstereotyped Negro drama have about converted the official American stage to the proper portrayal of the Negro. This is a lesson, however, that Hollywood has yet to learn. Despite their new medium, the movies are still wedded to reactionary social conventions which, unfortunately, give wide currency to outmoded Negro types and vanishing or unrepresentative social situations. Just recently, pressures of war propaganda have made a slight dent in this Hollywood tradition. Two musical productions in which some of our best dramatic artists have been cast have just finished production. These full length pictures Hollywood announces as "revolutionary." Actually they are not, but they do mark some break with Hollywood's intransigence and give some ground for hope in the not too distant future.

It is in the fields of fiction and social analysis, finally, that most progress is to be recorded. Under the sobering influence of the economic depression, and, too, of the wider vogue of literary realism the fiction of the

Negro life has been completely transformed in the last decade. Popular fiction, as *Gone with the Wind* and *So Red the Rose* at best, regrettably, still persists in the old tradition. But our real literature has long since repudiated such pride and prejudice. The accomplishment was not easy, however, for either the white or Negro writer. The one had to acquire more objectivity, the other deeper social vision and insight. Both, by now, have about succeeded.

Although exposing often the paradoxes and injustice of race prejudice, the Negro prose writers delineate both the northern city miles and the Southern peasant with careful often skillful objectivity. The capacity for this and for self-criticism represent a most desirable stage of intellectual maturity. Writers like Rudolph Fisher, Eric Walrond, Claude McKay, Langston Hughes, who has written a novel,—*Not without Laughter* and a book of short stories,—*The Ways of White Folk*, Zora Hurston, Walton Turpin, Richard Wright prove this accomplishment. The latter's *Native Son*, Book of the Month Club choice a while ago, is really one of the great sociological novels of our generation.

As for the white writers, there is an increasing vogue for a serious and sympathetic treatment of Negro themes and the Negro's problems. Much of this has come recently from Southern writers, a promising symptom of growing liberalism. A whole generation of young Southern novelists, Robert Rylee, Hamilton Basso, Wm. March, James Childers, Josephine Johnson, Minnie Hody, Julian Meade have succeeded the path-breaking older realists,—Clement Wood, Stribling, Sherwood Anderson, Faulkner and Erskine Caldwell. They are presenting at last a fully humanized Negro and an honest and frank description of the Southern social scene. Like those equally frank critical analyses of Cash's *Mind of the South* and Jonathan Daniel's *A Southerner Discovers the South*, this new liberalism breaks sharply with Southern traditions and prejudices and raises a common cry for social, economic and spiritual reform.

Southern literature today is several steps ahead both of current Southern public opinion and social practice. So is careful sociological scholarship in its analysis of the Southern scene. From the Negro research centers of Howard and Fisk Universities, from much general centers as the University of Chicago, the University of North Carolina and its well-known press, and lately from the American Youth Commission an increasing number of objective studies have come describing and diagnosing our American situations and maladjustments of race and race relations. Foremost to be noted, after the unimpeachable objectivity and frankness of most of these studies, is the fact that of ever-increasing productivity of Negro scholars in the various fields,—sociology, history, economics, combined with a growing tendency to collaboration between white and Negro analysts in this special field. The ten volumes of the American Youth Commission Studies and the projected ten-five already published of the Carnegie-Myrdal study of the Negro in America are about evenly divided between white and Negro research scholars, another sign, I take it, of significant cultural progress.

We have here, it is true, an advance which only as yet affects the respective elites of the two race groups involved in our North American civilization. The next step, as well as the problem of the moment, is the practical use of this new understanding as instrument for social enlightenment and constructive social reform. That, and some of its prospects we shall discuss in the next lecture. Thus far, we have seen that Negro influences and contributions have been marked both at the folk level and in the formal culture of the United States. We have stressed the formal contributions because the folk-gifts are nowadays so generally recognized and accredited. We should not underestimate the latter, for it is just as important, perhaps more so, to color the humor of a country, or to influence its tempo of life and feeling, or to mold its popular song, dance and folktale, as it is to affect its formal poetry or art or music.

Certainly it is to be expected that the combined influences of such contributions will eventually bring about a new cultural appraisal and fuller social acceptance of the Negro in North American life. The country has at least never spurned the Negro's cultural gifts or been cold to the spiritual elements of our racial temperament. This destroys once and for all any thought of the Negro as a nation within a nation or even as permanently to be shut off in a cultural Ghetto. In view of the integral character of the Negro's culture with that of the dominant majority, and especially in view of the complementary character of the Negro traits with those of the Anglo-Saxon Nordic, it would seem to be a situation of profitable exchange and real cultural reciprocity. For the Negro's predisposition to the artistically creative and his spiritual sensitivity make him a desirable and needed factor in our American cultural life. But we must conclude by saying, with all the force of historical and moral logic combined, that on today's advanced and democratic level it should be, nay, is impossible to accept a group's cultural products and reject the producer, praise and prize the one and deprecate the other. On this the teaching of the facts is clear and unequivocal, and so at least the intelligent elite in my country anticipate and strive toward fully realized cultural democracy.

NOTES

1. Quoted in Locke, Alain. "The Negro's Contribution to American Art and Literature," *The Annals of the American Academy of Political and Social Science* 140 (1928): 234–47. 243.
2. Hughes, Langston. *The Weary Blues.* New York: Alfred Knopf, 1929.
3. Toomer, Jean. *Cane*, New York: Boni and Liveright: 1923.
4. Cullen, Countee. *Color*, New York: Harper and Brothers Publishing, 1925.
5. Edward "Abbe" Niles. "Introduction," in *Blues: An Anthology* edited by William C. Handy. Bedford, Massachusetts: Applewood Books, 2001.

Lecture 4: The Negro's Sociological Position in the United States

We now turn to the consideration of the sociological position of the Negro in the United States, which concerns primarily, of course not the peak-line advances of the elite but the base and the median lines of the condition of the masses. The racial situation and its prospects depends as much or more upon these facts and circumstances as upon the success and achievements of the leaders. Nevertheless, the rapid development of a competent elite and the psychological effect of its advances have given both guidance and inspiration to mass progress. But the only right and democratic solution of what we have now for generations called, somewhat unintelligently, as we shall later see, our "race problem," rests fundamentally on the satisfactory improvement of the socio-economic conditions, the civic rights and the educational and cultural opportunities of the great mass of the Negro people in our country.

We recognize at the very outset that this is one of our gravest national problems, and that though great progress, educational, economic, social, has been made by the Negro minority since emancipation and moderate progress in the change of attitude of the majority population toward this racial minority, there nevertheless remains a serious discrepancy between our North American creed and code of democracy and our actual social practice of it with respect to the Negro. No intelligent or honest American would deny such a fact, and in increasing number now begin to see the futility and lack of social wisdom in attempting to evade or ignore the issues it raises.

© The Editor(s) (if applicable) and The Author(s) 2016
J.A. Carter, *African American Contributions to the Americas' Cultures*, DOI 10.1057/978-1-137-56572-3_5

And so, to the extent that time allows we proceed to discuss it,—let us hope, frankly, objectively, intelligently, constructively. With particular reference to the latter, let me add that this is my main reason and justification for discussing it so largely in terms of the immediate present rather than the historical past, likewise for treating it in the context of democracy and our present world conflict for the safety and security of that same democracy. This, I take it, would also be your prime interest in the matter. More than mere statistics, you will want to come to know the situation in terms of its trends, and above knowing something about the issues, you will want to know what can be reasonably stated as to their prospect of solution. This, then, I may assume is our task.

Some statistics, especially of extent and rate of the Negro's social, educational and economic progress will be necessary, but on the whole we shall be discussing trends and controlling factors. Indeed, the statistical figures most needed are not yet fully available from the 1940 Census, which is so elaborately analyzed as to take even in normal times several years after the enumeration for detailed analytical breakdown. These figures alone can give us the accurate scientific picture of the state of the Negro population, for everyone admits that the Negro's progress during the last decade, including small increase in relative proportion to the general population and very considerable decrease in mortality rates, has been phenomenal and beyond previous statistical predictions. At present these thirteen millions constitute nearly 10 percent of the total population, are in a condition of unusual mobility from South to North and West, the Far West now considerably included, are rapidly centering in cities-almost half now live in cities, and will of course be further considerably changed and shifted by the rapid and deep reaching changes of the present war. One can readily see what was meant by saying that the situation was changing even while we discussed it. More than that, some significant statistics that are already available involve themselves with war statistics and the prudent necessities of the national defense.

However, it is more important for the information and understanding of an intelligent layman to consider the situation in its general aspects, its main trends, and its promises for the future. Based on these facts, we can identify three specific trends of significant transformation of our racial problem, as it stands today. Competent and judicious observers admit the following three perspectives:

(1) That when the situation is analyzed more realistically and objectively, the more it shows aspects of a social and economic problem, seriously affecting not only the lives and happiness of the Negro minority, but the overall improvement and evolution of the majority of the population, particularly in the South.

(2) That in view of the constant movement of the Negro population and development around urban areas, it is no longer a regional problem, which must be left to the control of limited regional arbitration, but rather a general problem whose solution requires a national context for its progressive solution.

(3) Finally, that it is no longer a purely domestic problem, because of the consequences and objectives of the current war programs, on the contrary, its happy solution determines the foreign policy and the moral authority of the United States of America, if it is to become the spokesmen and champion of democracy.

During our discussion, I will try to explain and justify the three different interpretations, indicating what may be their influence on the present state of things, and hence on the hopes of the contemporary generation of American Negroes. What was during the campaign against slavery, primarily a moral purpose, and was unfortunately, during the period known as Reconstruction, an interregional political matter between the North and the South, has become a serious problem, both social and economic, which is now developing into a national problem. This difficult situation is not without consequences for the international life and prestige of the United States.

We will not make reservation, raising an issue that is related to the war undertaken for Democracy. This is one of the inevitable consequences of our time. On this question lies one of the new aspects of the whole problem, and at the same time, the hope of its practical solution. For it is inconceivable that one of the largest and most advanced democracies, can allow social or economic problems to arise between it and its absolute capacity to organize the war within, and demonstrate its full moral authority abroad. On the first point, it is to be noted that already for war efficiency Federal, that is to say national, legislation and Executive Order of the President have been called into action to curb racial discrimination in war industry and the like. The Order #8802, creating the Fair Employment Practices Committee, has already brought about unprecedented employment of Negros in plants, even whole industries and in semi-skilled and skilled gradings previously barred by local custom and private policy, all over the country, South as well as North. Included in the scope of this order have been those race discriminatory practices of certain labor unions themselves as well as the policies of employers. These gains, made under the pressure of war emergency, may not remain completely after the war, but they will have transforming effect on one of the main causes of the Negro's present disabilities,—unequal chances in employment and economic opportunity. War conditions are therefore forcing a more liberal and more uniform policy throughout the nation in these respects.

On the second point, our leading statesmen, who happily at this critical junction of the country's history are convinced liberals and prior to the war were even advocates of constructive programs of social and economic reform, have publically admitted for a national practice of democracy without exception or reservation whatsoever. They stand for putting our democratic house in order, and understand that world leadership in democracy must be moral leadership and cannot accrue to any nation which cannot abandon racial and cultural prejudice. And in complete agreement on this point, I ask permission to quote from a recent publication in a leading journal of liberal American opinion these words of my own:

> The international front of race has been permanently joined to our home front of race, and only a consistent, fundamental policy seems possible. All the more reason, then, why hoary traditions, already internally inconsistent, should be uprooted when they stand between us and our goals in war and peace. We must, therefore, put our democratic house in order, and drop those racial differentials which amount, after all, to a double standard of democracy.
>
> Here in the United States, in 1860, fate cast the Negro in the role of a test case of the basic human right of freedom, of the integrity of our National Constitution, of the Union. Today the Negro is cast in an international role involving on a world scale pretty much the same issues of political morality. The Negro's cause becomes the fulcrum of this extension of democracy, a world hostage to its prospective fulfillment.[1]

This is one of the realistic reasons why it was stated at the beginning that in the light of present circumstances the Negro minority question is equally a matter of the concern and welfare of the whole nation and of the basic interests of the white majority. There are other internal reasons that will later be discussed leading to the same conclusion.

But now let us look for a moment inside the black minority life itself. Here, too, we find a transformed situation. Here we no longer see a disorganized and unenlightened peasant mass inertly acted upon by majority policy and discrimination. We also witness a considerable disappearance of that condition typical at one stage of all oppressed minorities where the blindly emotional resentment of prejudice and injustice results in confusion and internal factionalism over ways and means of remedy and of group program. Competent observers agree that the Negro minority in the United States has about passed this stage and is now not only fairly well organized and responsive to intelligent leadership but in many ways positively unanimous as to basic objectives. Fortunately these objectives are none other than those of the Constitution and Americanism, as we call it, itself. What some short-sighted observers regard and deplore as a sudden intensification of the race problem is nothing more than the inevitable increased pressure of rapidly accelerated Negro progress and more firmly consolidated assertion and mass opinion of the minority. There has been a marked increase recently of unanimity and basic agreement both among the leaders and among the Negro masses; in fact some of it among the leaders has been forced upon them as they have sensed the growing solidarity and conviction among the masses.

It is always a significant turning point in the minority group's social history when such a consolidation of opinion and purpose takes place. From one point of view it is even more important than material progress because it mobilizes that progress and focuses it toward basic collective ends. Naturally such agreement cannot be upon any one specific program or formula of race solution; it is rather an agreement to struggle by all possible ways and means to the now commonly understood end. The most potent single factor in this social development of the North American Negro has been an enormous spread and improvement of the Negro press, which functioning democratically even in wartime, has become almost without exception a courageous, vigilant and well-informed champion of minority rights and stimulator of progressive minority effort. Ahead even of any statistics of specific progress, it is my duty to report this significant fact. Because of it, we may definitely predict that the Negro's own attitudes will play an increasing role and have larger effect in the equation of racial adjustment in the United States.

This factor, too, the war cannot help but intensify and stimulate. Apart from the general repercussion of wider mobility and wider economic and social experience on the part of the home population, we must realize what a considerable transformation of viewpoint and experience will result from the discipline of military training and the contacts and lessons of overseas service upon the youngest section of approximately one-tenth of the Negro population,—for it is no secret that the Negro is sustaining his proportional fraction of responsibility in military service of one kind or another. Indeed, in previously barred or limited branches of military service, the Navy, the Marine Corps and military aviation, extensions of Negro eligibility and participation have been put in force, much of it on the initiative and pressure of Negro public opinion. These considerable contingents will return not only deserving more of our democracy but expecting more, and it is idle to think that in a democratic system this will not have revolutionizing effect. More concretely even, many of these Negro soldiers, disenfranchised contrary to national law by local state legislation or electoral practice, have been invested by national war legislation with the franchise and will vote from all over the world in the 1944 elections. Again, it is unthinkable that they will contentedly return to their former subordination and disenfranchisement, or that, with the new organic consciousness developed in the group nationally, their racial brothers in states where they already exercise the ballot, sometimes with a balance of power, will not bring a perfectly legitimate and peaceful weapon to bear upon this situation. Of course, one must repeat, that is only upon one premise that it is profitable to discuss the situation at all, namely that of victory for the democratic nations and our maintenance, therefore, of the democracy we have. For if not, under fascism, whether imposed from within or without, most of us, even the white majority, must count on experiencing conditions equal to or worse than those of the most oppressed sections and classes of the Negro population. Though related to fundamental principles and moral sanctions of democracy, this is predictable realism. It justifies our statement, I believe, that the democratic context of today introduces a new practical force and hope into our problem of race. Not only is the conscience of the majority more fully aroused as to what democracy should mean, but they are in a position to see more realistically what its denial to others also means. Not only is the minority more united, informed, and aware of its traditional rights guaranteed by the Constitution, but it realizes that the trends of the past work inevitably in its favor. Now, before analyzing the social and economic factors that bring new perspectives to the racial situation, I would add a final statement regarding the psychological condition of the Black minority.

All minority situations, in both their affirmation of ideas and their program of action, oscillate between the need for a practical compromise and radical claims of rights and principles. We have already seen how this has in the past divided the leadership of the Negro group, by a controversy between the so-called equal rights schools and the so-called compromise and conciliation school of Booker Washington. Today, representative Negro thought is in a distinctly militant position, and in a phase that involves no compromise. It is not that they are determined by the war, but the consequences of the war, however, make it an inevitable and natural extension of democratic principles. Both Negro thought and experience have realized the ambiguity of an accommodative policy toward the principle of segregation or any other project of biracial organization in a common national existence.

Dr. Abram Harris, a prominent economist, demonstrated definitively the aberrations of a biracial economic regime and he masterfully denounced the mistake of any entrepreneurial project that would be based on a distinction between black and white, and that would establish economic affairs for Whites separately from Negroes. Among our sociologists, E. Franklin Frazier and others have not only exposed the handicaps of our minority, but also the public dangers of the racial division of society into different residential neighborhoods. They concluded that segregation has never favored the development of equality, but it is doomed to establish instead a system of perpetual inequality. The facilities in existence have never been equal in practice, and therefore the famous formula which promised equality in segregation, proved an illusion. Especially in the economic, but also from the educational point of view, it has never been possible to obtain equal facilities for Whites and Negroes. The organization by the big factories and department stores, of separate Negroes only housing, rendered commercial success impossible despite a few Negro companies. The segregation in housing and schools has always given the Negro poor living conditions and poor conditions of education, without exception, wherever the system was used, whether in the North or in the South. There is an approximate equality and joint institutions in the region from Northern Washington D.C. to the west of Cincinnati, and in the Mid-West and Western Kentucky. But beyond this area public institutions are again separated between the races. Yet virtually no Negro authority accepts the principle of segregation, even when forced to resign himself in practice. We can say that segregation is accepted only under duress, but it has never been tolerated and is constantly fought.

There still endures in Negro public opinion, another harmful division: the color prejudice that even as it tends to disappear, exists among the Negro themselves and functions as a sort of internal projection of the outside prejudice of the majority, which separates people who are lighter skinned from those who are the darkest. The fact that the North American racial prejudice makes no difference in treatment between blacks and mulattos is certainly against this distinction, and other internal constructive forces gradually correct this handicap which constituted at one point, a serious obstacle to the unification of the group. Under the pressure of contemporary events, this division seems about to dissipate, as the gap was filled in gradually during Reconstruction, between the newly emancipated slaves and free men of color who were already numerous enough. Everyone now recognizes that the liquidation of this problem is inevitable and necessary. But it has already had a serious effect over cooperation, despite manifesting itself as social snobbery. This is an all important factor in the progress and development process of a healthy and moral minority, and absolutely indispensable to the interior organization of Democracy.

This racial self-deprecation finds its extreme manifestation in the practice of "passing," as it is called,—the practice of some Negroes, indistinguishably fair, to lose or deny their racial identity to enjoy the privileges of being white. This is a social phenomenon badly needing understanding on both sides of the color line. In the first place, not all of it is psychologically race treason or race denial. Some of it is just pragmatic crusading, using a natural weapon against racial prejudice with definite intent and justification. Much of such action is clandestinely explained, and known to darker, more obvious Negroes. Considering the immediate advantages, the marvel is that there is proportionately so little of this, with thousands of fairer-skinned Negroes constantly loyal at great personal cost to their racial affiliation. The Executive Secretary [Du Bois] of the largest civil rights organization among American Negroes is a man indistinguishably white, with blue eyes, who has always to announce his racial identity where not known personally and who, until his photographs were circulated, used frequently to investigate lynchings and other racial disturbances by direct conversation with their perpetrators. Time and again in the South fair Negroes submit to "Jim Crow" accommodations and treatment from a sense of deliberate group loyalty rather than fear of detection.

"Passing" seems to us and to many peculiarly Negro because of the matter of complexion and what has been called the Negro's peculiar index of group visibility. But this is a general phenomenon of social oppression and inter-group prejudice. With other groups subject to social persecution and ostracism, there is similar behavior, with slight difference of degree and discoverability,—witness the frequent phenomenon of the distinguishing of characteristic minority accent, the alienation and disowning of peasant parentage, the plastic surgery on a tell-tale racial feature, or even the protective conformity of the apostate Jew, the over-Anglicized Irishman or Hindu or the over-Gallicized African. However, let us in remembering the outraged indignation of the "respectable" Irish over the Irish folk theater in Dublin of 1910 what to them was "a representative and shameful past," let us recall that that revived peasant tongue is now the official language of Eire. Like the epidemic rashes, of childhood, these reactions are the unfortunate hazards of cultural childhood and adolescence. There is no sound maturity or progress for a minority group, however, until such a period and its group illnesses is successfully passed.

With these indications of the typical state of mind in the minority situation, we will briefly consider new perspectives in social and economic terms. As we have said before, the migration of the Negro was his most effective weapon. With such great differentiation in the tradition and customs concerning racial problems that exist in different regions of a vast country, it has always been possible for the Negro to change, as an individual, his social climate. Some thousands of individuals have realized this, and tens of thousands promote the idea of a single migration. Although it often intensifies racial tensions in the better districts toward which this migration flows, it usually produces only reactions of attitude not of basic social conditions. Communities after all rarely are so resentful as to set back their clocks of progress on account of the Negro, though exceptionally some of them do. The new migrants pay a considerable toll, often through slum crowding, but they pay the price willingly and rarely return. For most of them it is a social gamble resulting in a half to a whole generation's progress by the mere stroke of moving. It is our generation's analogue to the fugitive slave and the "Underground Railroad," only now it is open and above board, and there is no democratic way of stopping it.

This internal migration, even within the confines of the South, usually means a change from a rural to an urban situation, with the southern city often only a half-way stop from which the migrant or some of his children finally land up in some Northern, mid-West or even Far West center. The Negro populations of New York and Chicago have increased a third and those of Detroit, Cleveland have doubled within the last decade. In that same period there has been a 25 percent increase in migration to the North and of 42 percent in the migration trend to the West, and quite half of the whole Negro population now lives in cities. We can get some idea of what this means sociologically if we contrast the possible extremes of variation to be gained by a migrating Negro farm peasant within the range of two to six-hundred miles, which incidentally is a small fraction of the 3000 mile long diameters of the United States. He can change from a racially segregated school system to a mixed one, from farm shanty to paved streets and electric light, from Jim Crow cars and no public recreational facilities to common use of parks and all public facilities, from a four month ungraded school term and no compulsory school attendance to a nine month graded school system with compulsory education up to 16 years, from a vote-less peon to an enfranchised voter after 6 months to a year of residence. The inequalities show what are the basic social problems and needed reforms of the South, where the majority of the Negro population still resides,—but of that later. The facts make for the peculiarity of our minority situation. In other countries minority situations, where they exist, are relatively uniform all over the country, often with the borders closed. The leverage of the variations of our racial situation is considerable, most effective of all, the lever which is in the Negro's own hand, the right of internal migration. Southern communities, feeling the loss of their labor supply have occasionally had to meet this by improving local discriminations, but with their set tradition only by timid and often grudging relaxations. This is what was referred to when I spoke earlier of the importance of the factors of internal variation.

Naturally this means that the city Negro, and especially the Northern and Western city Negro, are the present pivot of race progress, and as well these are centers of race leadership and militancy. Their types differ radically from what is conventionally known as the typical Negro, and so great is the force of the migration that the picture of even the mass Negro must soon be altered. For the fundamental changes come from an urban, industrial exposure and affect the ordinary worker nearly as much as the educated middle class. Even as far back as 1920, as a result of the first war migration in Chicago the percentage of Negroes employed in manufacturing industry rose from 3 to 11 percent and the proportion of semi-skilled workers rose three and a half times in that decade. The Negro in the United States has a foothold in the most modern type of Western industrialized civilization, and will be well-rooted in it when the unprecedented gains of the present war come to light. All we know about them now is that they are proportionately much greater.

It is this present labor front which is most important in the present stage of the struggle. Much effort is being directed, with justification, toward opening wider the door of economic opportunity, now only half-opened.

Great credit must be given to these sections of organized labor who see clearly the connection between admitting the Negro worker on equal terms in the common interests of the worker's welfare. Both by its principle of organizing all grades of workers and also because of more liberal racial policies, the C.I.O.—Congress of Industrial Organizations has recently contributed much in this line. The older labor organization, American Federation of Labor has an inconsistent policy, admitting Negroes in some crafts and excluding them in others. They face now, however, not only the strong competition of the C.I.O, but the new government ruling against discrimination at least in war industry. The Negroes admitted under this emergency situation to labor unions will of course never leave them in any great numbers. In one aviation plant, as an instance, where the policy was not to employ Negroes in skilled trade work, the number in skilled employ rose from zero to a thousand; in another Southern shipyard, the threat of C.I.O. organization of the plant forced the conservative A.F. of L. to change its policy of excluding Negroes. These are single instances, but they are indicative. There is growing recognition, particularly among Negroes who were previously apathetic to labor organization because of the labor union policy toward them, that a standardized pay and working conditions spell industrial democracy. And among the workers generally there is growing too, the realization of what it means to all of them, black and white, not to have sub-standard labor competition.

More and more the realistic understanding of the situation is not in terms of racial situations but of basic socio-economic factors and conditions. Of no situation is this truer than of the South's situation itself. It has taken years for this realization to come about generally, although Booker Washington pointed it out clearly 3 decades ago when he said: "You cannot hold a man down in the ditch, without staying down there with him." Liberal thinkers, Southerners included, now recognize and admit this, and regard general economic reconstruction as the only solution for the problem of the South. The general non-progressive character of the South is a definite consequence of reactionary policies, many of which are primarily entrenched in racial discrimination and the tradition of keeping the Negro down. But the lesson of the situation is that such systems, if allowed to continue and become chronic, spread beyond the group for whom they were primarily intended. The so-called "sharecropper" problem in the South is by no means racial; it affects an estimated—millions of poor whites as well as—million Negroes.[2] There is no hope, as the Southern Farm Tenant Union sees it, of improving conditions for the one without doing so for the other, and so, their basis of organization is interracial. In Birmingham, Alabama, similar enlightenment on a skilled labor industry, coal and steel, have broken down local tradition and resulted in mixed labor unions. The condition of the sharecropper, white as well as Negro, is so bad that for him even migration is pretty well out of the question. His prospect of hope is in one or other of the phases of the federal government's program of farm rehabilitation, and this, being under federal auspices, is being applied with very little or no racial discrimination. It is the only hope of the South in this its most basic economic activity and its gravest single social problem. The hope of getting the Negro peasant back on the farm depends upon its development, for once having tasted even unskilled and casual labor conditions in the cities, those who have been able to migrate steadily refuse to return. The greatest experiments in planned social democracy seem due to be worked out in the South; here again not from philanthropic motives, or even directly as an attempt at solving a racial situation, but from the pressure of definite common needs. All such generally administered reform programs, such as federal programs must necessarily be, will be of great benefit to the Negro. The national housing program, as an example, after considerable opposition, has just succeeded in allotting the Negro about 12 percent of its new housing facilities, a slightly higher proportion it will be noted, than his population ration. But that, I take it, is on the same supposition by which we must overfeed undernourished children because of the pitiable lack of modern, sanitary housing for much of the poor Negro population. Progress is doubly difficult because of the inability of the average man in the street to understand either the necessity or the justice of this. Questions of racial psychology do, therefore, enter in as complicating factors, but the problems and any really fundamental solution must be worked out on a more objective and humane basis.

A singularly interesting case of this involves the program of practicalized vocational education which Booker Washington worked out at Tuskegee as his solution of the Negro's problem. It turned out not to be a special remedy at all but an important contribution to American educational techniques and methods in general. On the one hand, it was years after recognized as one of the first vindications of what is now practiced generally in the States as industrial training or vocational education as an integral part of the public school system. It was thus a real contribution to American educational theory and practice. On the other hand, it proved only a part solution of the problem of the Negro's educational needs, for just as much, if not more race progress has pivoted on the higher collegiate type of training leading to research scholarship and the learned professions. From that we have recruited our most pioneering and some of our most effective leadership. The only sensible conclusion being, of course, that both types of training are needed, and that educational programs developing under private initiative and missionary auspices, as did originally all schools for the Negro in the United States, the South especially, for their eventual fullest social effectiveness need to be converted into standardized, publicly supported education. Many of our schools are thus being consolidated, the University of Atlanta now consolidates four schools started originally under separate denominational auspices, one Baptist, one Congregational, one Methodist, one African Methodist; and many originally private institutions are now public.

Not only is wide improvement in public educational facilities necessary and basic in the South, were the average expenditure for a Negro child's education averages only $17 to a general average for the education of the white child of $50 per capita, but federal subsidy toward equalization and improvement of southern school facilities is regarded as the most immediate practical remedy. A federal bill toward this end, and, with non-discriminatory provisions, has been pending for several years: it at least has back of it the endorsed support of liberal educators and professional educational organizations. With the base-line of Negro education as low as it is, it is all the more remarkable that Negro enrollment in public high schools (secondary education) has increased fourfold between 1920 and 1930, and more than doubled again between 1930 and 1940. Enrollment in colleges beyond secondary education, as our school system goes, is estimated between 35,000 and 40,000 with college and professional graduation now annually between 3,500 and 4,000 in round numbers. Our advances in research scholarship can readily be statistically understood by contrasting the total output of doctors of philosophy up to 1915 as 10 with what is now an output in the last decade from 8 to 15 annually. With no Negro institutions yet giving such higher degrees the standardization of our scholarship at least at the top is self-evident, and indicative, too, of more democratic trends at the higher levels of the educational and intellectual life generally. Here again, as justifying our analysis of the situation as increasingly intersectional also in its constructive aspects, let us note that, just as in previous generations education for the Negro in the South was a product of northern missionary enterprise, so the standardization of the Southern collegiate training for the Negro today is the work largely of men trained in the North and Midwest who are products of the more democratic situation of mixed schools and generally open university education, while survey of the facts substantiates, it is to be hoped, our analysis of the present stage of the American Negro situation as neither a purely racial problem nor one that is or can remain a particularly sectional, local or purely domestic problem. The more we refuse to allow our minds to be blinkered by the old traditional and limited ways of looking at it, the less we shall be able to understand it or do anything constructive about it. These realizations are dawning in the most modern and liberal views, and if there is any one focusing conclusion of the many studies being made it is that, as has been once said, this racial question if fundamentally a socioeconomic issue to be solved only by rather generally applied socioeconomic programs and remedies. Viewed that way, the problem breaks down into a number of specific issues of social maladjustment and concrete measures of social reconstruction and reform. This approach also links up the effort to benefit the Negro and right his group injustices with all the national campaigns for practical and progressive democracy, such as the movements for better popular education, wider use of the franchise, labor rights, social security, farm reconstruction, civic improvement of sub-standard housing and living generally.

There is, and until better adjustments have been made always will be, special irony in the Negro's case as a group. For historically and culturally his is a very paradoxical position, and his case is a very deep challenge to our American democracy. For not only is he the largest, he is from the point of length of residence, the oldest of our minorities. Culturally, as having more marked commonality of language, customs, and traditions with the majority than any other minority group, he should not normally be subjected to the sharpest differential treatment. Our national history also reveals the Negro as one of the most loyal and serviceable of the country's constituent stocks. Six thousand or more Negroes fought in the War of American Independence in 1775, 200,000 fought on the side of freedom and the Federal Union in the Civil War of 1880, 400,000 in the First World War, with a minimal expectation of double that number in the present struggle. Negro opinion generally, for these very logical reasons expects and anticipates full democratic equality of treatment. On that very score it is emphasizing less and less special legislation or specialized social programs as the means thereto: the appeal is more and more to general principles, and of course, as the mainstay of our democratic society, to the Constitution, which as many of our leaders are prone to say only needs to be enforced and implemented to solve what is known as the "Negro problem."

Any realist, however, will face the fact of an imperfectly realized democracy in many other respects in our present-day society. Indeed as democracy realizes itself by stages, the racial shortcomings are but part, though a vital part of the agenda. The same racial situation which is admittedly part of the pathology of the democratic process can and should be constructively used, as it has already in the past, as an index of diagnosis and healing reform. There was lately a bill in the United States Congress about an obviously desirable democratic political reform: it was the bill for the abolition of the poll-tax, which restricts the voting of thousands of poor whites in a number of the Southern states, though it is one of the effective means of Negro disenfranchisement. It was introduced by a liberal Southern senator, though defeated in the Senate after passage in the House by recalcitrant reactionary Senators from the same section; some of them motivated by the determination not to see the Negro a step nearer enfranchisement and the democratic power it would bring in its train. As a publicist wisely commented;—the more racial discrimination, the less general democracy. Fortunately, I think, this case is typical. It does not present us with an impending feud between black and white or the progressive protagonists of black man and white man, but between progressive friends of democracy and reactionary traditionalists, the division of opinion within the same section, namely the South, that in last analysis must be so pivotal in any successful solution of our race minority issue. That South which confronts us with the undemocratic phenomena of lynching, segregation, chronic exploitation also in terms of its progressive elements presents us, happily, with at least the beginnings of progressive farm and industrial unionism, broadened franchise, social and economic reconstruction programs of the sort already mentioned. It is on such grounds that, accepting this perspective of optimism, I termed, with deep, personal conviction, the American race problem as part of the unfinished business of democracy.

NOTES

1. Locke, Alain. "The Unfinished Business of Democracy," *Survey Graphic: Magazine of Social Interpretation*, 31:11, (1942): 455–461. 459.
2. The typescript has dashes where these two figures should be included and the final French version which Locke delivered does not indicate the actual figures either.

Lecture 5: Negro Achievement in the United States

Having surveyed the cultural and the sociological position of the American Negro, it is now a pleasant duty to particularize in terms of a somewhat more concrete account of typical achievements in the various fields of civilized endeavor. Here again, a statistical account might first come to mind, but necessary as factual accuracy is, to give that merely would be only to present the bare skeleton of our minority group progress. Especially since the progress that has been made needs to be measured primarily in terms of the handicaps and obstacles which have been overcome, it seems best to introduce the human dimension into the picture by presenting this group progress symbolically in terms of thumb-nail sketches of typical personalities and their individual achievement. Thus will we be able to sense, I hope, the human drama as well as the special import of this rather epic and certainly inspiring accomplishment.

North Americans of today measure progress, their own as well as that of others primarily in materialistic terms, and that indeed is the natural emphasis of an age of industrial expansion and scientific technology. The Negro group, for various reasons, has been particularly handicapped in opportunity along these lines, though as we shall later see, the limited opportunity in industry, business and technical skills is gradually being removed. The Negro's first lines of significant advance had perforce to be along spiritual and artistic lines, because these were fields more subject to internal control and less dependent on efficient and dominant group organization. There may have been an additional reason of group predisposition toward the artistic lines, because these were fields more subject to

© The Editor(s) (if applicable) and The Author(s) 2016
J.A. Carter, *African American Contributions to the Americas' Cultures*, DOI 10.1057/978-1-137-56572-3_6

internal control and less dependent on efficient and dominant group organization. There may have been an additional reason of group predisposition toward the artistic and the spiritually creative, but the success of our youngest generation with experimental and exact science, and its growing lean toward technological interests, engineering and aviation particularly, caution us against any hurried generalizations of that sort. Indeed two things are to be borne in mind about this anyway. The keys to civilization and progress are after all spiritual, and the base of all forms of progress rests on the control and discipline of the mind and the means for the mastery of the art of thinking. Historically the base of our great North American achievements in civilization were laid down, generations in advance of the industrial era, by the spiritually minded and education-centered culture of New England that founded our great universities and modeled our democratic ideals. Be that as it may, the progress of the Negro necessarily had to pivot on the struggle for education, first the right to have it and then the fight to obtain it. And so it seems to me that the most significant single set of statistics in the whole of the Negro's progress are those that tell, on the one hand of the reduction of an illiteracy of 85% in 1865 to an illiteracy of only 9% today, and on the other hand, of a positive type of educational progress represented by 55,000 Negro college graduates with over 40,000 now studying in colleges and professional schools. For this indicates three things at once,—the capacity for the mastery of the basic means of civilization and culture, a somewhat solid and rapid educational accomplishment, but more significantly, still greater potentialities. In this light the drive of the aspiring classes of the Negro may be understood as not just a fanatical overemphasis on formal education but the desperate struggle toward the most promising and least impeded path of progress. The Negro, because of the restrictions of prejudice and limited practical opportunity has had to over-qualify to get a chance at all and has been forced to follow first the lines less open to organized resistance.

With this in mind, we turn now to a review of some of the major fields of human endeavor to illustrate typical Negro progress and how it has overcome many of the traditional and even present handicaps. We shall have to be brief necessarily if we are to pass in review the full gamut of activities, including the more recent developments in business, technology and applied science. So, in turn, we shall take the fields of music, art, literature, scholarship, race leadership, labor organization and social work, the field of woman's work, religion, research science, technical science and the applied science of agriculture. Here, certainly is a representative range, if perchance, in the time at our disposal we can give any enlightening account of it.

Music is easy to start with, because it is a field in which everyone knows of the Negro's facility and success. One may profitably wonder why? To my thinking not because he was any more musically endowed, but because here is a field too close and intimate to be blocked by any prejudice and too direct in its appeal to be stopped by any man-made barriers. Even taking away his language and all the externals of formal culture did not close fortunately this one remaining avenue of free expression. And so the Negro sang—at least—freely, long before he had any other freedom than that of emotional expression. We have already spoken of the Spirituals: they are the fruits of this one undeniable freedom, even though the products of a slave experience. A brilliant ex-slave once called slavery the "graveyard of the mind"—incidentally it was Frederick Douglass who said that. Fortunately it was not also a tomb of the spirit. But it is interesting to note in passing what brought the spirituals to their present position of world attention and favor. A singing troupe, starting out in 1879 to campaign for funds for a new building for Fisk University captured its audiences with these songs after they had first experimented with the classical musical taste of the day. Net result,—not only fame for the singers, including a command performance for Queen Victoria in England, but after several tours funds amounting to $150,000 and Jubilee Hall for their struggling college. Time and again, as the Negro climbed to toward recognition as a serious musician the same formula has had the appeal to the less racially prejudiced reactions of Europe to be repeated. For only the acclaim of the leading music circles and critics of Europe brought about the recognition of such now outstanding singers as Roland Hayes and Marian Anderson. But the door pried open by this leverage was easier to open another time, and when presented to the general public in 1940 by Koussevitsky, Dorothy Maynor, our latest singer of stellar rank was accorded instant recognition of a sensational kind. Previously, indeed, she had been soprano soloist with the famous Westminster Choir. With Paul Robeson this group ranks without reservation in the public mind as front-rank national artists, with Miss Anderson only behind Toscanini, Heifetz, Rachmaninoff and Horowitz in income and audience rating. The insistence of their reputation has taken these artists into the heart of the South, where they have equally found favor and cordial reception to the point where several of them have successfully stipulated modification of Southern traditions of segregations at their concerts. Normally one does not expect music in the role of social reformer, but it is a part of the romantic story of the Negro musician. The same social suasion may be credited, in its own way, to the jazz vogue, which has gradually democratized its audience in many ways, including the now readily accepted arrangement of mixed jazz orchestras, after Benny Goodman's brave experiment of this character. When classical jazz was first presented in 1922 in Carnegie Hall, Paul Whiteman and George Gershwin were the sponsors. It was a great event and contribution, but 20 years after, last January, an even more significant and democratic event took place in the same sacrosanct Carnegie; Duke Ellington's twentieth musical anniversary gave the Negro jazz musician and his band the highest musical accolade in the gift of our public, and with it a testimonial scroll signed by thirty of Americas leading musicians, among them Damrosch, Roy Harris, Toscanini, Stokowski.

The musical career that I would like to thumb-sketch, however, is of a less known name. But is even more significant, representing the not merely as recognized musical interpreter or even as jazz composer but as composer in the classical forms. It is the quietly startling career of Wm. Grant Still, born in Mississippi but now resident of California. Beginning with recognition by his fellow musicians of the League of American Composer, Still's chamber music compositions from 1924 on have been gradually placing him in the front ranks of creative American music. His two symphonies, played now with reasonable frequency and his orchestral-choral ballads of recent years have solidified his outstanding position. The two latter beautifully symbolic, in that they are two libretti written by Katherine Chapin, in private life, Mrs. Francis Biddle, wife of the present Attorney General. One is on the racial theme, a choral lament entitled "And They Lynched Him to a Tree," with obvious liberal import and the other, "Plain Chant for America," is an even broader and more general plea for paramount democracy. The huge popular success of these, with the publicity of Mr. Still's winning of the prize for the theme composition of the 1939 World's Fair in New York, have brought general acclaim to what was already in professional musical circles an established reputation. This leaves only one round of the musical ladder to be scaled by the advancing Negro musician, the stage of the Metropolitan Opera, and word comes recently of a next season's contract for Paul Robeson to sing the Boris Godounov role in Russian at the Chicago Civic Opera.

Let us turn briefly to the field of art. Here we have always had single outstanding talent, even as far back as 1800, when a Negro portrait painter, Joshua Johnston was doing commission portraits of Maryland notables, and worked competently enough for some of his canvasses to have been attributed to Rembrandt Peale before later authentication as the work of Johnston. Or again, we have the exceptional career of the early Negro sculptress, Edmonia Lewis, sent to Rome by the abolitionist Story family in 1865 and the acceptance of Wm. Bannister by his fellow artists of Providence, Rhode Island, a decade later. However, to my thinking the significant point that should be reported in the evolution of the Negro artist is neither this, nor the sensational and international ovation, which was made in Paris for the late Henry Tanner in the last century. The real success was achieved five years after 1929, when the works of Negro artists were fully recognized as a coherent expression of Negro life, but even better as a vital part of American artistic movement. The assiduous campaign in New York and Chicago produced this outcome despite a certain indifference and a powerful opposition. Beyond the merits of the artists themselves—a really outstanding young generation full of talent and originality—great credit goes to the Harmon Foundation who organized for five years, exhibitions to showcase the work of Negro artists, as well as Federal Committees Supporting Artists, which were a real nursery for twenty of our youngest and most representative artists. As an example of this last fact, we must remember the phenomenal career of Jacob Lawrence who, at the age of sixteen attended a Federal Committee Workshop to assist artists in Harlem where he received his first and most unique training. I remember his first sketches on brown wrapping paper, which shows a beautiful perspective after eight years in the remarkable triumph of which I have already spoken; his obtaining the sixth highest purchase price in the National Competition organized by the Metropolitan Museum. The work of the remarkable Negro sculptor Richmond Barthé obtained the same place in the competition. Richmond Barthé is currently exhibited in more than a dozen of the best American museum collections, and has always preferred Negro type subjects without thereby confining himself to them exclusively. I think his personal career is also symbolic. Born to creole parents in New Orleans, his talent was discovered by the parish priest, at which point he was sent to study at the Art Institute of Chicago. There he worked doubly hard in the Art School program during the day and as a food service worker at night. His talent as a sculptor was revealed on the occasion of the search for works to promote the Negro in Art Exhibition, organized in 1928 by a bi-Racial Committee in Chicago. Since that time he has developed a maturity and has become one of the best known among our contemporary sculptors. At the entrance to Central Park in New York, at 110th Street, is his Memorial to James Weldon Johnson, one of our greatest Negro poets; and at the entrance on Fifth Avenue and 101st Street, is shown in a rather ironic way, his memorial plaque, dedicated to Arthur Brisbane, famous columnist for the Hearst Press Syndicate, neither of whom are known for their sympathy to the Negro cause.

Considering now literature, we find, in one form or another, a continuously important phase of Negro life. Poetry, especially as early as 1775, with the work of Phyllis Wheatley, the first remarkable poetess of our Negro group, and second poetess of the nation, has always been an important means of expression. Then came polemical speeches and essays, which for obvious reasons of race management and defense, were also a popular genre. In these fields, we not only supplied our quota, but we usually had distinctly great representatives. However, the Negro's literature really reached its fullness in his efforts to relate strictly racial slogans and objectives into national letters, at the time of the "New Negro," movement in 1925. For it is from this time that our writers were deliberately thrown in the mainstream of American literature, repudiating racial propaganda in favor of individual expression. Since then, our writers have struggled to comply with certain forms of literary style and a philosophy that began with the aesthetic movements of the 1920s and 1930s.

Today, two trends dominate among most Negro Writers: a southern regionalism and a proletarian or Marxist realism. We will consider briefly one representative of each of these trends. The signs of these trends are reflected in the work of Langston Hughes, but Sterling Brown is probably today's outstanding exponent of the Southern school and Richard Wright, certainly, of socialistic realism. Brown, born in Washington, only on the boarder of the south, deliberately spent ten years teaching at various institutions in the deep South to have a vantage point to study Negro peasant life and its idioms. Consequently, both in his verse, his literary criticism and in his forthcoming folk-study of the Southern Negro, he presents us the best available literary documentation of Negro peasant thought and life as it is today. Wright however was not only born in Mississippi but as a vagabond youth experienced this life not only firsthand but with all its hardships. Still without much formal education, he has become an outstanding American writer with his sensationally successful novel of Negro life in Chicago, his short stories of equally vehement social protest, *Uncle Tom's Children* and his drama of the novel, *Native Son*, which after Broadway successes was presented on tour from New York to the

Far West. With a great gift of style, Wright can so successfully dramatize the hard facts of the average Negro's life as to make even a shocked and unwilling public listen. *Native Son*, with the large initial reading public guaranteed by its selection by the Book of the Month Club, may yet be the *Uncle Tom's Cabin* of this generation: if not, most people expect some such general result accumulatively from the work of Richard Wright, at least if his talent fulfills its initial promise. But Negro realism is rarely as drab as realism normally is; for it is generally shot through with poetic imagination even at its grimmest. Stellar instance of this is another rising poet, who won this year's Yale University Prize for contemporary younger poets. She is Margaret Walker, southern-born, western trained, a college teacher of English, but for all that a singularly original and unconventional type of poet. The volume in question speaks her viewpoint in its very title;—*For My People*—she calls it very simply. But it is a ringing challenge to present-day America, indeed to the whole world, since her basic credo is not merely democracy for the Negro but democracy for all the oppressed and socially disinherited. "Let a new earth rise" she sings, "Let another world be born. Let a bloody peace be written in the sky ... Let a race of men now rise and take control."[1]

You will surely expect, in this running account, some overview of serious Negro scholarship, especially that large section of it which has analyzed the social scene and tried to throw a light into the dim corners of the Negro problem. Here the first thing to note is that until recently, when scientific research is beginning to claim its share, the bulk of the Negro's scholarship has been forced to concentrate on racial matters. But just as in literature, we look forward to the time when such concentration will not be needed, and when the whole range of scholarship opens out before the younger Negro scholar merely in terms of his own individual bent and interest. Indeed that is even now a growing trend: I can call to mind, five relatively recent doctorates in mathematics and the still more recent phenomenon of a Chicago lad attaining this mathematical degree at the precocious age of nineteen and proceeding this year to Princeton's erstwhile sacrosanct School of Advanced Studies for further mathematical training under Einstein and Alexander. One can point too to increasing frequency of a specialization in chemistry, physics, engineering.

But for the longest while, and at some considerable cost of overbalance, Negro scholarly effort had perforce to concern itself with sociology and the race problem. Beginning with sporadic but credible efforts even during the anti-slavery period, this important phase only took on organized competence and objectivity with a generation of scholars still living, Dr. Du Bois and Dr. Woodson. The former founding some thirty years ago the first systematic series of social studies and the latter about twenty-five years ago the best of our historical studies, still regularly appearing each quarter, *The Journal of Negro History*. These two senior scholars, as has already been mentioned, pioneered us safely into the paths of sound and recognized social scholarship. It was not an easy accomplishment, especially as they had to challenge and refute so much pseudo-scientific information and theory about the Negro. That meant being racially minded without, if possible, being racially biased: an extremely difficult combination to achieve. Their great service was to have succeeded in just this, clearing the way for more detailed and specialized scholarship of the younger generation. Then, if it may be mentioned, came intermediate task of my own generation of scholarship whose main objective was to temper the militant racialism that had inevitably begun the crusade, and give in cultural racialism a broader, more humanistic rationale to our racial thinking.

Today, our youngest generation in these social studies are doing more than throwing scientific light on the race problem; they are making substantial contributions to the theories and techniques of social analysis generally. One can mention Charles S. Johnson, who as director of social studies at Fisk University is a leading researcher and consultant authority on the socio-economic problems of the South. Then there is Dr. Charles Wesley, of Howard University, whose study of *The Collapse of the Confederacy* demonstrated such ability to be objective on a difficult subject; Franklin Frazier and Abram Harris, sociologist and economist respectively of the same institution, whose studies also have been recognized as substantial general contributions to their respective fields. One need only mention in passing, Rayford Logan, already known to you because of his special interest in the historical study of Haitian-American diplomatic relations, and Eric Williams, who should be known to you as an authority both in the history and the current problems of the Caribbean. And in a moment, we shall be mentioning one or two still younger scholars more particularly. But, with the mention of so many of my colleagues from Howard University, I am obliged to explain that this is properly accounted for by the fortunate situation of this particular institution, and are not matters of special wonder or credit but rather in line with its unusual resources. Of course, Howard University is only one of some four or five outstanding Negro colleges, but its location and equipment do combine with a substantial national subsidy to make it inevitably a leading center of

Negro scholarship. In its seventy-five years of existence, it has turned out nearly eleven thousand alumni, now graduates annually about 400 from a student body of over 2500, has a full complement of University faculties and technical departments, with combined faculties of over 250, a plant of ten million dollars valuation and an annual maintenance subsidy, not including student tuition, of about three-quarters of a million. This naturally determines a considerable educational and research output.

But I am anxious to hurry on to give some idea of the newer turns in the development of Negro scholarship. A few concrete examples will indicate them. There is now a slowly increasing number of Negro members of general college and university faculties; Harvard has one in medicine, the College of the City of New York has one in psychology; the University of Chicago, one in pathology and one in educational psychology. The latter is Allison Davis, the brilliant young anthropologist who collaborated on at least four of the Youth Commission studies of Negro youth. For some years now the part-time services of Negro scholars have been utilized for research and advisory service to the Federal government, a practice rapidly increased recently by the exigencies of the war program. It is with some pride that I can mention, now that the campaign in Africa is successfully over, that my colleague, Dr. Bunche, an authority in colonial administration, as a member of the Office of Strategic Services drafted some of the important technical memoranda of that campaign as the senior consultant of the Africa section. These facts indicate, I think, that we are thinking backwards in conceiving the function of Negro scholarship merely to be the teaching of Negro youth or the analysis of the race question.

In the previous lecture, we mentioned the importance of the labor and economic front. Here little seems to be known about the significant developments, some of them at the initiative of Negro labor leadership. The veteran labor leader of the group is Philip Randolph, who now in addition to being president of the largest Negro labor union, the Pullman Porters organization, is head of the March on Washington movement whose campaign for the fairer inclusion of the Negro in war industry precipitated the Presidential non-discrimination order already discussed. Later Negro labor leaders have tended to graduate from the ranks of labor, but here in this case was a white collar journalist who twenty years ago espoused the worker's cause. For ten unsuccessful years he campaigned before succeeding in getting official recognition of the American Federation of Labor for his union. But the struggle was worth the cost, for rapidly thereafter unionization of Negroes was undertaken both by the A.F. of L. and the newer C.I.O. The C.I.O. principle or organization is more liberal and democratic; its unions are interracial. The historical groundwork for mixed unions, however, was the pioneering precedent of the Mine Workers Union that became one of the first constituent unions of C.I.O. later. From the humble ranks of the democratic coal miners this principal is gradually spreading, and the work is in the hands of organizers, white and black. A singularly significant piece of labor reform, of great war significance though no war secret is the successful policy of the Maritime Seaman's Union. This union, with a mixed membership actually dictated a change in the policy of the ship owners against mixed crews, and has finally recruited almost ten percent Negro membership on those most important of all the sinews of the war effort, the merchant marine convoy ships; a feat of social engineering signalized recently by the manning of a mixed Maratime Union crew under Captain Mulzac, the first Negro shipmaster, Ferdinand Lewis, chief Negro organizer for this Union, is its national vice-President and a labor leader of general authority and counsel, as is also Willard Townsend, the Negro executive council member of the C.I.O.

As progress goes forward, the newer variety of Negro leadership becomes of this type of integration within mixed organizational ranks. However, there is still need for the continuance of the older varieties of racial organization and leadership. One of these represented by organizations expressly called into being for activities of interracial adjustments, like the Southern Interracial Commissions, the National Urban League and the like; the other, represented typically by the N.A.A.C.P. (National Association for the Advancement of Colored People), is of the militant protest type, which, though it may be bi-racial in organization, takes an unequivocal stand on a platform of principles and crusades for legal decisions or legislative and other direct reforms. Naturally both have their usefulness, but the continued growth, influence and success of the N.A.A.C.P. indicates clearly the public support and approval their type of program has among Negroes today. A hundred and fifty chapters all over the country, including now the South, a bi-racial board of legal advisers, increasing influence in national politics attest to its efficiency as do its seventeen legal victories in civil rights cases before the United States Supreme Court, usually after adverse decisions on the issues by the lower courts. Dr. Du Bois was previously the editor of its organ,—*The Crisis* and its executive secretary for a number of years was none other than James Weldon Johnson, the poet. Now Walter White, previously mentioned, is its vigilant and aggressive head. One of the most prominent of its legal counsel is Wm. H. Hastie, formerly Federal Judge of the Virgin Islands, and before that the solicitor of the U.S. Department of the Interior who drew up the precedent making articles of incorporation for the Virgin Islands Development Association permitting the investment of government capital in the promotion of civilian industries which might promote trade and general economic improvement. Mr. Hastie has until recently served as Civilian Aide to the Secretary of War, promoting and safeguarding the interests of the Negro contingents being drafted into the national armed forces. A political phenomenon with more than local significance also occurred in New York City recently. The Negro minister is by no means a new figure in political life, but far too much of that activity has previously been conservative and in alliance even with the reactionary forces of machine and old-line party politics. But Rev. Clayton Powell, pastor of the largest Negro Baptist church in that city, was recently elected to the New York City Council on the Labor Party Ticket, and with the third highest majority vote by proportional representation count, which of course, meant many more than merely Negro partisans.

Nothing is more characteristic both of recent national and racial developments in our nation than the increased participation of women in professional, political and civic welfare activities. Negro woman and their organizations, after a necessarily slow start, have been making tremendous strides in these directions. New York City, understandably in the vanguard in such matters, has for example usually women assistant district leaders of the electoral districts of both political parties, and has had two Negro women assistant district attorneys, one of whom served notably in the prosecutions of the anti-vice crusade, and now a young Negro women Judge of the Domestic Relations Court, Jane Bolin. Numerous younger women are entering the social work profession, both on a professional and a volunteer basis, and during the period of government relief, a Negro woman, Mrs. Mason, was assistant supervisor of the entire Manhattan program. Negro women have now for several successive terms been members of the state legislatures of Pennsylvania and Ohio, and from the frequency of their candidacy in Illinois and New York will undoubtedly make their debut shortly in these assemblies.

But, in spite of all this younger generation progress, anyone asked to name the outstanding symbol of the Negro woman's progress would agree on the name of Mary McLeod Bethune, now nearly an octogenarian. For fifty years she has been a pioneer in educational and woman's club organization work, having succeeded in building up by personal promotion along with many other activities, what is now known as Bethune Cookman College in Daytona, Florida. The rise of this school from two frame cottages to an accredited college of six hundred students makes Mrs. Bethune's life story a woman's edition of the life of Booker Washington, with the noteworthy exception that, instead of a program of conciliation, she has always been even in the heart of the Deep South a fearless militant. For the last nine years, in her late sixties and early seventies, she has directed this college and its fund promotion drives simultaneously with the administration from Washington of the Negro division of the National Youth Administration, a program at one time covering almost every state in the Union. Here, certainly, is a symbolic figure and a prophetically encouraging career, indicating the role that woman's initiative and influence is likely to play in the situation of race relations and progress. This is all the more significant if we take into consideration the well-known fact that women's organizations in the United States have within the last ten or fifteen years been more liberal and militant with regard to race issues on the whole than their corresponding men's organizations. This statement includes the Young Women Christian Association, the Women's League for Peace and Freedom,—whom you may remember sent the Balch Commission to investigate the American occupation of Haiti, woman's professional associations, etc.

Negro business enterprise is one of the most difficult of all aspects of our group life to give accurate account of. Yet it is, of course, or rather has been until very recently the most emphasized and typical of all American interests. Negroes have encountered an unusual amount of handicap in anything but small merchandizing and proprietary businesses, and in spite of frequent campaigns have for various reasons not been able to make startling gains, except by way of some few notable exceptions like the North Carolina Mutual or Victory Life Insurance Companies, each with volumes of business necessitating several millions of reserve capital. The main reasons have already been indicated, the futility of a separate business economy with the large scale organization of business and business competition typical of our highly industrialized national economy. The incorporation of the Negro both on the employment and investment sides of American industry is necessarily slow, but eventually inevitable. Negroes, distracted for a generation or so by the hopes of independent business development, are just beginning now to use their organized consumer power to force consideration in the higher ranks of business employment and opportunity. Campaigns for "buy where you can get a job" and for higher rank employment in public utilities and the activities of advertising and sales-manship have recently resulted in marked, even unexpected gains. For the competitive character of many of these concerns forces a change of policy in most of them, once one concern has capitulated to consumer or public opinion pressure.

There is another bright hope on the economic horizon, and that is the increasing governmental control to which first the depression and then the present war are subjecting what we have for so long termed "Big American Business." Very little Negro business has developed to such gargantuan proportions as to need control, but the operation of present and forthcoming business controls will undoubtedly favor Negro business enterprise and facilitate the progressive incorporation of the Negro into the economic side of our national industries. For more and more it is gen-erally becoming an employment rather than a promotion problem. The conservative policies and traditions of private enterprise will have to yield, not only this point of better proportional Negro inclusion, but on the gen-eral question of collective bargaining, systematic upgrading of employees, fixed minimum wages and working regulations, and for the public services, supervised employment policies. As benefiting far larger numbers and as having more effect on average income and living conditions, such pros-pects are more encouraging for a minority group than any possible spurt in big business investment and control. Yet the record, against odds, of the successful promotion of such Negro corporations as the North Carolina Mutual or the million dollar publishing plant of the Baptist Publication Society of Nashville at least demonstrate executive business skill and initia-tive. And as indicating what can happen in enlightened business initiative when capital does suddenly become available, I should like to cite two interesting cases. One was the recent action of a Philadelphia Negro fam-ily suddenly in possession of a quarter of a million: their investment was in a model low-rent housing project for their less fortunate brothers. The other, a case that has had profound repercussions on public opinion; the man who as Rochester is Jack Benny's foil comedian, from his large but not too socially constructive earnings as Edward Anderson is proprietor of a large parachute manufacturing company with a laudable mixed racial employment policy in his large and growing concern.

We now come finally to that other phase of North American specializa-tion, science and technology, in which the Negro has had so notoriously so poor a start. It may seem curious to begin at the pure science rather than the practical end, but I need only ask you to imagine what might have been the possibilities of economic wealth and control among Negroes if Jan Matzlinger, the Negro who invented the lasting machine, basic technological instrument of the modern shoe manufacturing industry had been able to hold his interests and dictate employment or investment policy, or if Elijah McCoy, another Negro, inventor of the mechanical lubricating cup had received his fair share of this basic technological improvement.

The Negro scientist and technician both because of changed attitudes and conditions, is struggling for more equitable integration in the scientific and technological activities today. He is not always in the scientific and technological activities today. He is not always receiving it readily, but the struggle goes on encouragingly, as a few type cases will illustrate. Let us begin with a career that was a mixed triumph and tragedy—that of the late Dr. Ernest Just, one of the most eminent experimental biologists of this generation. While teaching at Howard University, he became internationally known among his fellow's scientists for his research publications in fertilization and cell physiology. Not until after his foreign calls as visiting researcher at Dahlem Imperial Institute, Berlin and the Marine Biological Station at Naples, and an unaccepted call to become vice-director of a Physiological Research Institute in Moscow, was he made a vice-president of The American Association of Zoology. And although consulted frequently from all over the country by fellow biologists, few of them could invite him to return to lecture or teach at their own institutions. He might have chosen to remain at his post at a Negro university, but the fact that he never had the opportunity of refusing calls to the greater research facilities and the wider influence of the general centers was of course, as I have already indicated a tragic loss of both a national as well as a racial character. Despite his outstanding success, the big opportunity of his life came too late. Eighteen months ago, when he himself was dying of cancer, came a hasty summons from a Cancer Research Commission to become a research associate to work out the possible clues that his latest publications had suggested to these medical research scholars.

But we proceed with two or three more cases, each with its lesson in some respects more hopeful. The career of George Washington Carver has made a profound impression, especially since his recent death and the publication of his biography, upon American lay opinion. The almost melodramatic episodes of his life, as one who rose from the status of an ex-slave to that of one of the great American pioneers in chemistry and scientific agriculture, helped dramatize his significance. So, too did his own self-sacrificing devotion to teaching at Tuskegee and his refusal of fabulous offers to go elsewhere in the research employ of various industrial concerns interested in the commercial exploitation of his discoveries and techniques. His custom was to go for consultation, south as well as north, and return either with empty pockets or a check that he turned over to the Carver Fund for student scholarships. Here was a career that probably will in the long run have revolutionizing effect not only on stimulating the interest of Negro youth in the possibilities of technological research and discovery but in widening the opportunities for Negro participation in these all important phases of our civilization. I have time only to quote from a recent *New York Times* review of his biography:—"His early studies of the Leguminous, or nitrogen producing plants popularized the peanut crop in the South and introduced the Soybean in America. From the peanut, he derived such unlike products as cheese, beverages, washing powder and synthetic rubber ... His discoveries in fact are almost endless. Some of them, for example, the large scale use of dehydrated foods, which he developed, we are only beginning to catch up with now under pressure of war necessity." It was Dr. Carver's fixed philosophy of life that anything that would permanently help the Negro must basically help the whole South, and he lived to prove it and see that general truth accepted. For much Southern recognition came to him, especially as the man who in the time of the devastation of the cotton crop by the boll-weevil, had suggested the constructive remedy of crop differentiation and founded the lucrative peanut growing industry as a practical way out.

Our next case has its own irony, but also its positive constructive side. At the very time when there was furious discussion going on over the biased and scientifically discredited policy of the American Red Cross in segregating blood donations from white and Negro donors,—a practice not yet officially disavowed despite protests of the American Medical Association and other scientific authorities, a young Negro blood research specialist, Dr. Charles Drew, was called to New York to take charge of the laboratory experimentation on the stabilization of blood plasma for war use. Its long distance shipment had developed certain technical difficulties of deterioration. Dr. Drew is publically credited with such successful solution of those difficulties on the part of the laboratory staff which he supervised that it is regarded as one of the major contributions of the medical war effort. For by his plasma reduction methods and controls, dried blood plasma can be shipped in unlimited quantities by airplane without deterioration and with standardized stability of type. Still in his mid-thirties, Drew is one of the vindicating talents of the rising young Negro scientist, as indeed is also a somewhat older medical research personality. Dr. Augustus Hinton, for years attached to the pathological research department at Harvard's Medical School, the inventor of the Hinton reaction test for syphilis, which is generally being adopted as the most reliable test in this important field of medicine and public hygiene.

One final case, the most encouraging, it would seem, of all, if we take into account, as we should, the necessary broadening of opportunity for the regular participation of the Negro scientists and technologists in American science and industry. Oddly enough in the very field of Dr. Carver's basic discovery of the food value of the soybean and the possibility of its American cultivation and use, which he communicated immediately and modestly to the U.S. Bureau of Agriculture, if today one were to visit the research laboratories of a large multi-million dollar industrial company in Chicago, chemically exploiting the many subsequently discovered uses of the soybean, one would find in charge of their soybean research division, Dr. Percy Julian, former head of Howard University's chemistry department. Dr. Julian, research chemist of Harvard and Vienna training, indicates a gradual but one hopes increasing use of the Negro technician in the applied as well as the theoretical aspects of science. Certainly since this is one of North America's great emphases, and has and will be one of our outstanding national contributions, race progress for the Negro must cross this barrier in ever-increasing measure. The general public is hardly aware as yet that it can or has been done, but the informed and inspired section of Negro youth know it, and are setting their goals accordingly.

NOTE

1. Walker, Margaret. *For My People*, New Haven: Yale University Press; First edition, 1942.

Lecture 6: The Negro in the Three Americas

It seems fitting that our final consideration of the Negro in American life should be set in the broadest possible perspective, and so I propose as our final subject, The Negro in the Three Americas. Even should we discover no further common denominators—though I think we shall—there will be at least two of great contemporary concern and importance,—Pan-Americanism and democracy, with both of which the general situation of the American Negro has, as we shall try to show, some vital and constructive connection. Our opening lecture, indeed, suggested that the furtherance of democracy in this Western hemisphere was bound up crucially with basic social and cultural policies upon which Negro life and its problems had direct bearing. It is incumbent upon us to justify such statements.

But before coming to the discussion either of theory or policies, let us first consider facts. In the United States of North America, we are well aware, sometimes painfully so, that the very presence of a Negro population of nearly ten percent of the total populations constitutes a race problem of considerable proportions. I am aware, of course, that under an Anglo-Saxon regime of race relations ten percent may constitute, indeed does constitute more of an active problem than a considerably larger population ratio would generate under the more tolerant Latin code of race which culturally predominate in Central and South America. However, what may show up very clearly on the surface of our North American society as a race problem may to a degree also be present under the surface of large areas of Latin-American society as a class problem, as we shall later see. At any rate, as to

© The Editor(s) (if applicable) and The Author(s) 2016
J.A. Carter, *African American Contributions to the Americas'
Cultures*, DOI 10.1057/978-1-137-56572-3_7

the facts, a larger proportion of the Caribbean and South American populations is of Negro racial stock than even our North American ten percent.
On a mass statistical average, by conservative estimates, the Negro population ratio of the Western hemisphere, the USA included, is 14 percent,
and the closer we come to the mid-zone of the hemisphere the higher that
proportion becomes. For the Caribbean or West Indian islands, it is 46 percent, for Brazil it is estimated at the lowest as 28 percent, by some as high
as 36 percent. Columbia is more than one sixth Negro, Ecuador fourteen
and Venezuela more than eight percent. The Central American republics,
except Cost Rica, have their considerable Negro admixtures, Panama especially. Indeed of all the American nations, only Chile, the Argentine and
Canada can be said to have a negligible concern in this particular issue of
race relations. Indeed when we superimpose the figures of the Indian population—so considerable an element in all Central and South American countries—and then the large East Indian or Hindu populations of Trinidad and
British Guiana, we begin to realize and appreciate more the polyracial character of our Continent and the fact that this phase of human group relations
is more crucial and critical in our inter-Continental life and its progressive
development than in even our respective national societies.

Fortunately, although different specific measures may be required, the
same basic attitudes and principles of fully democratic living will resolve any
of these problems, one as well as the other. They have different numera-
tors and degrees in color differentials, but they have a common denominator of arbitrarily limited and unfulfilled cultural and economic democracy.
Certainly for such a population situation, whether it be upon the basis of
caste or of class, a hegemony of white or even the fairer elements of the
population cannot be made to spell real or effective democracy. Nor can
the group attitudes involved be forged into any really unified and durable
hemispheric solidarity. It is in this way, to anticipate our analysis somewhat, that these matters condition Pan-Americanism almost as critically as
they limit expanding democracy.

It is the common historic denomination of slavery which despite all
other difference of national culture and social structure has determined
both the similarity of condition and the basic identity of the problems
which still so seriously affect the Negro population groups of the American
hemisphere. For they are all the cultural consequences and economic
aftermath of slavery, and like slavery itself they must eventually be completely liquidated just as that institution was itself abolished. Slavery in
America was, of course eliminated at different times and in quite different

ways: here in Haiti, that came about by means of a slave rebellion; with us in the United States, it was Civil War; in still other American nations, the process was legal emancipation, in some cases gradual, in others, immediate. But the lives of most persons of Negro blood and descent in America directly or indirectly, in one fashion or another or one degree or another are still seriously affected by the cultural, social and economic consequences of slavery. By an approximate estimate this involves at least 35 million of human beings among the total American population of 266 million, among these the 13 million Negroes of the United States, the 12 or more million Negroes in Brazil and the 8 or more million Negroes of the Caribbean.

To be sure, a considerable and an encouraging number of these Negroes have already attained the average level of cultural status, and a certain few have raised themselves considerably above the average levels of their respective cultures. But it should be clearly recognized that so long as the masses of these Negro groups comprise, even in part as a consequence of slavery so heavy a percentage of those who are illiterate, undernourished, ill-housed, underprivileged and in one way or another subject to social discrimination, just so long will it be necessary to give serious consideration both to the special causes and the specific remedies of such conditions, and to take stock, as well, of the undemocratic social attitudes and the anti-democratic social policies which invariably accompany these conditions.

Having now before us the fundamental historical reasons why so large a proportion of American Negroes enjoy less than their proper share of democracy, whether we take stock of the situation in Baltimore or Bahia, in São Paulo or in San Antonio, let us consider some basic common reasons why they must eventually share more fully and equitably in democracy's benefits than they do at present. The reasons which we have in mind to consider are not the uncontested and incontestable arguments of moral principle and abstract justice—important as they may be—but certain very particular and realistic reasons which it seems wise and opportune to stress at this critical hour of human history and social development. Doing so concretely, and on a hemispheric rather than a narrow nationalistic basis may reinforce their timeliness and urgency. One nation cannot directly solve the other's problems, but certain important international dimensions have lately come into the general area of these problems which should prove mutually reinforcing and helpful. It is profitable also to see the Negro population and its claims in the same perspective.

In the first place, in every one of the countries where he constitutes considerable proportion of the population, the Negro represents a conspicuous index by which the practical efficiency and integrity of that particular country's democracy can readily be gaged and judged. For the same high visibility which internally makes possible ready discrimination against Negroes makes the domestic practices of race externally all the more conspicuous and observable in the enlarging spotlight of international relations. However fundamental the domestic issues of race may be, today and for the future we must all be particularly concerned about their international consequences. This holds in general on a world scale. Here the American treatment of the Negro can have and already has had serious repercussions on enlightened Asiatic and African public opinion and confidence. Or, for that matter, so will our treatment of any racial minority such as the treatment of American segments of the Hindu or the Chinese resident among us. But this situation holds with intensified force as between the Americas and with particular reference to the widely distributed American groups of Negro and mixed Negro descent. For historical and inescapable reasons, the Negro has thus become a basic part and conspicuous symbol of the cause of democracy in our Western hemisphere.

For the United States, especially interested in and committed to a program of broader and closer Caribbean cooperation as well as to a thorough going furtherance of Pan-American solidarity, the foreign frontier race, so to speak has become more critical even than the domestic. Fortunately this is being seen and realized with increasing force and frequency by enlightened liberal opinion in the United States. Far-sighted statesman and progressive race leaders alike realize that sounder and more consistently democratic practices of race at home are necessary for the successful prosecution of these important foreign programs and essential as well to complete conviction and moral confidence in our democratic professions and intentions. The "Good Neighbor" policy has worked a miracle of political and economic rapprochement between the Americas, but democratic race equality and fraternity, as its morally inescapable corollaries are practically necessary re-enforcements of the "Good Neighbor" policy and principle.

This situation, as an acute observer has recently stated, is not altogether unilateral. Latin America has its part to play in the developing American democracy of race. This observer, my colleague, Dr. E. Franklin Frazier, has the penetrating view of the situation to offer on return from a year's study and observation of the Caribbean and Latin America. Although he finds that the race barrier to American solidarity stands to the credit side of the more favorable and democratic character of the typical Latin attitudes toward race, he also observes that Latin America has her important part to play in the achievement of racial democracy. "Differences between North and Latin America," he says, "in their attitudes toward race constitute one of the real barriers to American solidarity. This is a question that has not been faced frankly in most discussions of Pan-Americanism." "But," continues Dr. Frazier, "one might add that on the part of Latin Americans as well as of North Americans there has been a tendency to evade the issue, though their conflicting attitudes toward racial mixture are the basis of a real distrust and lack of mutual respect. In their dealing with North Americans, our Latin neighbors have often been careful not to offend our feelings with regard to color caste. This has been facilitated by the fact that the ruling classes, with some few exceptions, have been of predominantly light complexion. But (and I stress this but), as the masses of these countries begin to rise and as there is greater intercourse between the Latin-American countries and North America, such evasions in the long run will be impossible."[1]

Professor Frazier has put his finger on the crux of the issue, but in a practical and constructive as well as acutely diagnostic way. For if at times class differentiation and its prejudices have contrived to aid and abet outright color caste prejudice, there is the obvious necessity of reinforcing democracy from both sides of this as yet admittedly unsolved social and cultural situation. The situation on either side needs and ultimately must undergo considerable democratizing. Almost all America, one way or the other and to one degree or another, suffers yet from the unhappy consequences of slavery, which in one situation has left us an undemocratic problem of class and in another, an even less democratic situation of color caste. We shall discuss this situation again a little further on, but it is worthwhile in passing to note the disastrous negation of democracy possible if, by way of the shortcomings of democracy either in the South or the North, fascism and its attendant racism should gain firm rootage in American soil. For then, as has been said already, racial and minority disabilities will have become a majority predicament and a general democratic catastrophe.

We must now hurry on, since ours in the constructive motive and interest, to sketch what favorable cultural trends are today coming to the aid of the cause of race democracy. But since slavery is the common root of our present difficulties, North as well as South, and in the Caribbean most especially, let us take one final backward glimpse at slavery itself in its most fundamental relationship to the whole American social scene. In the first place, it is salutary to recall that it was only historical accident that a white indentured servant class did not bear the brunt of the labor load of the European settlement of this continent, and thus become the victims, if not of slavery, certainly of its close equivalent. One need only remember the indentured servants, the convict debtors of the early United States colonies or the Jamaican Irish similarly imported as a laboring caste. However, through slavery and the slave trade, this hard fortune but constructive contribution fell to the lot of the Negro. In so doing slavery did two peculiar and significant things which have determined the course of American history and influenced the character of American civilization: first, American Slavery, since it was of the domestic variety, planted the Negro in the very core of the dominant white civilization, permitting not only its rapid assimilation by the Negro but it's being, in turn, deeply and continuously counter-influenced culturally by the Negro; and second, it also planted the Negro—and that holds true for today as well as for the past, at the moral and political core of a basically democratic society, so that around him and his condition wherever there are undemocratic inconsistencies, must center the whole society's struggle for the full and continuous development of freedom.

As we shall more and more realize, the extension of American democracy must involve the reversal and eradication of these historical consequences of slavery, and it is more than appropriate, indeed it is morally inevitable that an historical American ill should have, in the long run, a typical and successful American cure. This is what I was thinking forward to when I said in the third lecture of this series that the majority stakes in the solution of the American race problem were nearly as great as the Negro minority's, and in the first lecture hinted that it would appear that the cause of the American Negro still had a constructive contribution to make to our current crusade for democracy.

We now come to some concluding considerations of ways and means. Especially important, it seems, are cultural developments, since they throw bridges of understanding and sympathy over the crevasses of the slow filling in of social reform and the still slower upbuilding of economic progress. They are essential, too, to the right and ready understanding of whatever group progress is being made along any other line. For some time now, undoubtedly, we have been aware of great Negro progress in our respective national areas, and have been taking national stock and pride in it. Now however, it seems high time to become more aware of it, as of other aspects of our American life, in an inter-American perspective.

All along it has been the tragedy of Negro talent and accomplishment to be considered and discounted in its full meaning as a matter of exception. It is only when added up and dramatically collaged that its proper significance is arrived at and its legitimate social effect brought to full realization. The cultural achievements and contributions of American Negroes, startling enough within their national boundaries, are from the approach of the whole hemisphere more than trebly inspiring and reassuring. In 1818 a French libertarian, Abbé Gregoire, inspired incidentally in great part by the galaxy of Haitian heroes of your Wars for Independence, wrote a small book on De la literature des Noirs, which proved one of the most influential documents of the anti-slavery campaign. For to the conviction of the Negro's moral right to freedom, it added in intellectual circles the demonstration that he had the capacity to fully use freedom's advantages. For so, in their brief day and as exceptions, these cases had previously been dismissed after the customary nine days' wonderment. But Gregoire added up a convincing total when placed beside Toussaint L'Ouverture and Phyllis Wheatley and Benjamin Banneker, the Maryland inventor, mathematician and almanac maker of Jefferson's day, the lesser known figures of Juan Latino, the sixteenth century Spanish African poet, Pareja and Gomez, the Negro painter-apprentices of Velasquez and Murillo, Capitein, the Dutch African theologian, Gustavus Vassa, the English African essayist. Together they were convincing justification of the Negro's possibilities and rights.

Though needing, let us hope, no such extreme conversion today, the intelligent and forward thinking public of the Americas needs reinforcing evidence of the present cultural attainments and growing cultural influence of the American Negro. It must come, too, with that overwhelming effect that can only derive from corroborative evidence from every quarter and from every one of the American nations having any considerable Negro contingent. Certainly such evidence is rapidly coming in, and it seems to reflect only our naturally limited information if such cultural progress seems to be more developed in North or South or Mid-America. Someday, and as soon as possible, it is to be hoped the general record will be compiled in its hemispheric rather than just a narrow nationalistic scope. Someday, too, and as soon after the conclusion of the war as possible, it is also hoped that inter-American exhibits and visits will make wider known and reciprocally appreciated the contemporary personalities and contributions of this cultural advance of the various contingents of American Negro life.

Here only in the barest outline can we begin to indicate them. But even that should prove enlightening and stimulating. Again, but this time on an inter-American scale, let us glance briefly at the Negro in music, art, folk-lore, literature and social leadership. Surprise is in store for any persistent student of the subject: I vividly recall my own, even after some years of reading, when I received unexpectedly the two volume study of Ildefonso Pereda Valdez of Uraguay on the influence of the Negro in the Plata Valley region, and again when Captain Romero turned up in Washington under the auspices of the Division of Cultural Relations of our State Department as an interested authority on the Negro in Peru.

To commence we may quote from a passage of Manuel Gonzalez, a statement that could easily be generalized to include also much of the Caribbean: "In Brazil, Cuba, Venezuela and other tropical localities, the Negro is the preponderant non-European race. The Negro is here, it is true, being slowly absorbed, but his deep inroads in the culture of these countries are today tantamount to a national characteristic and will persist for many generations to come."[2]

In music, paralleling the North American developments with which we are now already familiar, there are, of course, those rich Negro contributions of Brazil, Cuba, Trinidad and the French Antilles. Blending with Spanish, French and Portuguese elements, they have produced an extraordinary crop both of folk and sophisticated American music. First, we encounter pure or almost pure African folk forms, manifested in rhythmic forms accompanied by percussion instruments or drums only. Then came what Gonzalez calls "the mulatto expression"—the hybrid "Creole" forms which are mostly of popular appeal and significance, diverting and useful as he says in the widespread service of dance and popular music. In this field today the outstanding creator is the Cuban, Ernesto Lecuona, a close analogue of our North American Gershwin. Finally we have what for the future is perhaps most important, the symphonic developments based on Negro motives and rhythms, but harmonized and orchestrated with all the skill of the modern European tradition. Here, it is hard to say whether Brazil or Cuba is outstanding, for in the one we have the important work of Villa Lobos, Fernandez, and Reveltas while in Cuba we have Amado Roldan, Caturla, Pedro Sanjuan and perhaps greatest of all, Gilberto Valdes. The Brazilian group combines Indian and Negro sources, but the Cuban work reflects, of course, predominantly Negro idioms. Indeed some think that serious Afro-Cuban music is one of the most promising strands of our whole contemporary American musical development, and it certainly would have already been so but for the untimely deaths of Roldan and Caturla. Most of these composers cannot, of course, be claimed as Negroes, though several have mixed ancestral strains. That is not, indeed, the emphasis of our discussion: we are speaking primarily of the power and influence of the Negro materials. However, the situation does from time to time also yield a great Negro musician, like Gomez, or the Jamaican Reginald Forsythe, or one of the present musical lights of London, the Guiana Negro composer-conductor, Rudolph Dunbar. Add to this considerable accomplishment that of the North American Negro, and one has some idea of this incontestable domination for several generations both of American popular and serious music by Negro musical elements.

The situation in the field of art is also most interesting and promiseful. In the States we have undoubtedly among sculptors of front rank, Richmond Barthé, and of second magnitude Henry Bannarn and William Artis. The Cuban Negro, Theodoro Ramos-Blanco, is by general agreement one of Cuba's leading contemporary sculptors as is also his mulatto colleague, Florencio Gelabert. Professor of sculpture at the Havana School of Fine Arts, Ramos-Blanco is known both for his strong delineations of peasant and Negro themes and for his happy memorializations of Cuban heroes, among them his famous statue to the great patriot Maceo. Before an untimely death, Alberto Peña shared acclaim with Ramon Loy—companion figures in the sphere of Cuban painting. Indeed we may expect much of the development of the Negro subject and theme in Latin American art, whether it realizes itself in terms of the Negro artist or not. For already in Mexico, Rivera and Orosco have considerably emphasized the theme as has also Portinari, perhaps Brazil's leading painter. Gone completely, under the wide influence of these artists, is the over-Europeanization of sculpture and painting in progressive art circles in Latin America, and that automatically means the glorification of the indigenous types and instead of cosmopolitan emphasis, the people's norms of beauty. In countries where the classical tradition still hangs on, and where the native artists are convention-bound and timid, as once indeed were the North American Negro artists, that subject matter hold-back may be expected slowly to disappear. With it always comes a freeing of technique and stronger and mature accents of self-expression. Under the double leadership of North American and Mexican art that cultural revolution has already begun, and an art truly expressive of the polyracial elements in Latin-America, the Negro among them, may shortly be expected to show the effects of such influence.

It is in the field of letters that the Negro contribution has most generally expressed its unusual force in the Antilles and Latin America. Haiti, with its high and almost continuous tradition of authorship in *belles lettres*, with its successive schools of poets, usually far above provincial caliber and reputation, hardly needs to be told about this. Yet few of us, if any, realize the range and extent of the Negro's literary influence throughout the hemisphere, if for no other reason than the limited view imposed by four different major languages. But the record is formidable when we add up the Haitian, Cuban, Brazilian and North American contributions. Pireira Valdes *Anthology of Negro American Poetry* added even an Argentinean Eusebio Cardozo and a Casildo Thompson and the Uruguayan Polar Barrios and Carlos Ferreira. Most general readers do know of Brazil's leading contemporary novelist, Mario de Andradé, and can also name such first magnitude Brazilian writers as the poet and abolitionist, Luis Gama, Manuel Alvarenga, Tobias Barreto, one of Brazil's greatest poets, Cruz e Sousa and Machado de Assis, founder of realism in Brazilian literature. We need only in passing mention the brilliant North American contingent of Paul Laurence Dunbar, James Weldon Johnson, Countee Cullen, Langston Hughes, Dr. Du Bois and Richard Wright, to mention only the first-line representatives. And when we come to Cuban literature, only a book like Guirao's *Anthology of Afro-Cuban Poesie* will reveal the wide extent of the racial influence on both popular and academic poetry. But in addition, one has to take into account in the history of Cuban letters, Gabriel Valdes, better known as "Placido," Manzano, and especially the contemporary literary genius of Nicholas Guillen. With Marcelino Arozarena and Regino Pedroso, this almost dominates the present output of Cuban verse of distinction; surely, if we consider that the movement of folklorist expression is the produce of the initiative and labor of these three Mestizos. And then comes *Canapé Vert*[3] to swell the ranks of this growing current trend of literary interest and emphasis.

Nor has this creative literary expression lacked for critical support and backing. For years now in Brazil, Arthur Ramos and Gilberto Freyre have been issuing their scholarly studies of the Negro historical and cultural backgrounds, and similarly since 1906 in Cuba that tireless champion of Negro culture in Cuba's history and folklore—Fernando Ortiz, founder of the Society of Afro-Cuban Studies. For many of these years, too,

Dr. Ortiz has been promoting an even more important project—the closer relation of Afro-Brazilian and the Afro-Cuban studies. In this way, then, the new American criticism is actively promoting the appreciation of the indigenous aspects of our American culture, Indian as well as Negro, and laying the foundation for a much more democratic cultural outlook.

Best of all, Cuba and Mexico have both marshaled the reforms of their educational systems behind this movement, to the extent that in addition to a policy of wider public education, they admit the right of the people's culture to a recognized place in the program of studies. From such trends the various folk cultures must inevitably find greater representation in literature and the arts. So, if the folk yields have been as considerable as they have already been in spite of the discouragement of official philosophies of culture unfavorable to them, now that these policies have been reversed in their favor, they are doubly assured of enhanced influence and prestige.

Another factor needs, finally, to be noted. The cultural traffic that in the past has run so steadily from all our respective capitals back and forth to Europe now has swung around to a continental axis North and South. In these cultural interchanges, the native folk products and their representatives must be expected to play an increasingly important part. They are both more interesting, distinctive, and novel and, from the democratic viewpoint, more representative of the majority of the people. By the traditional exchanges in terms of stereotyped European models, we got only to know our outstanding artists as individual talents; now if they come bringing the folk culture, we shall, in addition, really for the first time be able to foster sound international and interracial understanding. And I cannot emphasize too strongly that these interchanges must be interracial as well as international, if they are to bring about the calculated democratic result. Elsie Houston and Olga Coehlo, for example, have really brought Brazil to New York in bringing their marvelous renditions of the Afro-Brazilian folk-songs: almost for the first time, do we feel that we have sampled the distinctive flavor of the national culture. Marian Anderson at this moment is making her first Mexican tour, another happy augury. And certainly one of the greatest needs in the situation is the one we have been prosecuting together so pleasantly and helpfully, for Haitian-American rapprochement is both an interracial as well as international undertaking happily so—not only for the two nations concerned, but for enlarging the democracy of the American mind throughout the entire American continent.

We might, indeed, close on this point of the radiant prospects for inter-American cultural democracy, but for a final, and let us say at the outset, more problematic point. Here, we must ask ourselves, finally, that other important question—what are the prospects for larger social democracy? Surely no one will claim that democracy can be complete or fully satisfactory without it!

Here the realism of the situation forces us to admit that unlike our cultural differences, which may even attract, our differences of social culture really do, in most instances, seriously divide. We know full well that there are great differences between the Anglo-Saxon and the Latin codes of race and the social institutions and customs founded on each. Not only do we have this as a matter of divergence between the Northern and the Southern segments of the hemisphere, but in the West Indies, we have these divergent traditions facing each other across the narrow strips of the Caribbean. But let us face the facts. Is there any way of looking at these differences constructively? Can we in any way relate them for the constructive reinforcement of democracy in America? At least, let us try.

The Latin tradition of race has, certainly, a happy freedom from *a priori* prejudice, looking at the individual first, and conceding him as an individual a reasonably fair chance. Triple heritage of the French Revolution, of Catholic universalism, and of Latin social tolerance, this is surely a basic democratic trait. The early and outstanding accomplishments of individual Negroes and their ready acceptance according to merit in Latin-American societies could never have taken place except on this foundation.

On the other hand, it is equally evident that the Anglo-Saxon code of race does base itself on a priori prejudice, and really, as the term itself indicates, pre-judges the individual on the arbitrary basis of the mass status of his group. It makes its exceptions grudgingly and as exceptions, and often cruelly forces the advancing segments of the group back to the level and limitations of the less advanced. Certainly no one would say it was justifiable either in principle or practice, no one that is, who believes basically in democracy. Nor can one say that it is democratic in intention: far from it.

However—and here I ask your patience for a moment—not as an apologist, God forbid, but as a philosopher, this hard code has had some unintended democratic consequences. In forcing the advance-guard of a people back upon the people, it has out of the discipline of solidarity forged mass organization for group progress. The successful individual in the majority of cases, still linked to the common lot, is not an élite released and removed from the condition of the rest of his people, but becomes as he advances an advance-guard threading through an increasingly coherent mass following. I am not condoning the circumstances which have brought this fact about; I repeat, I am merely describing objectively what has historically transpired.

Now let us put these separate pictures stereotypically together, to see if we can get a more three-dimensional view both of the situation and its prospects. The Latin-American code of race does more justice and offers less harm to the individual, but at the historical price of an unhappy divorce of the élite from the masses. The Anglo-Saxon practice of race seriously handicaps the individual and his chances for immediate progress, but forges, despite intentions to the contrary, a binding bond of group solidarity, an inevitable responsibility of the élite for the masses, a necessary though painful condition for mass progress. From the practical point of view, the more liberal tradition concedes but divides, while the other refuses to concede piecemeal, but by unifying, cannot possibly in the long run divide and conquer. This seems paradoxical, and is. But for one further moment, let us look at the history of the matter.

Both of these social policies of race, the Latin as well as the Anglo-Saxon, were laid down by slave-owning societies before the abolition of slavery. One saw in the more favorable condition and freedom of the mulatto a menacing advance that must be arbitrarily blocked by a solid wall of prejudice. The other for the most part, saw in the differential treatment of the mestizo the strategy of a buffer class, granting it considerably more than was allowed the blacks but always somewhat less than was standard for the privileged whites. Neither was democratic in intention or in the long run in basic historical effect. One produced an out-and-out race problem, the other, a tangential conversion of a large part of it into a class problem. Each respective group experience has something to teach, and the first common lesson is that you cannot expect to get democracy out of slavery or the institutional inheritances of slavery. We shall get along further and faster by the realization that democracy, as it must fully develop in America, cannot be developed either within the arbitrary and undemocratic traditions of color caste or fully within the less arbitrary but still undemocratic system of a racial élite split off, largely on the basis of a color class, from the race proletariat. Neither of these social race patterns of society is blameless, and to be fully democratic each needs radical improvement.

Obvious common sense teaches us that we shall only achieve fuller democracy in practice by democratizing further whichever system we have by historical accident inherited. However, in these days of international intercourse and collaboration, there are just as obviously mutual lessons which can be constructively learned and applied. One system, the Latin, has vindicated a basic essential of social democracy—the open career for talent and unhampered mobility and recognition for rising individual achievement. The other, the Anglo-Saxon, has taught an increasingly important essential of a democratic social order—the responsibility of the élite for the masses. The basic necessity of the latter, even within the Latin-American framework has been distinctly corroborated by the organization in 1931 in Brazil—a country where there is almost no race problem as far as the individual is concerned, of a National Union of Men of Color for the improvement of the well-being of the Negro mass population. It is the organization, which sponsored the notable Second Afro-Brazilian Congress 1937, and which, incidentally, in 1941–1942 played an important political role in Brazil's anti-Axis alignment against Nazi racism and fascism.

Instead of heightened partisanship over our differences of race codes and practices, it is quite within the range of possibility that, looking at matters more broadly and objectively, we shall move forward in our democratic efforts with a sense of collaboration and a common ultimate objective. For the more democracy becomes actually realized, the closer must our several societies approach a common norm.

Slavery is one of the oldest human institutions, nearly as old as man and nearly as universal. But the longest, the most extensive and the most cruel chapter in the history of human slavery is that dark African chapter of the trans-Atlantic slave trade precipitated by the colonial settlement of the Americas. We must never forget how substantially it helped to make the colonial conquest of the New World possible, thus laying the foundation of that American civilization which we all enjoy today. The slave trade involved the Three Americas. It has affected permanently both the population and the culture of the Americas; especially Mid-America. It has influenced the life of the Americas both for good and evil, and almost everywhere in America, to one degree or another, the shadow of slavery's yet incomplete undoing still clouds the possibilities of a fully democratic American society. Not only for the sake of that democracy, these consequences must be overcome. It is fitting and necessary that the inequities and human disabilities which came into our Western world by way of the exigencies of its colonial settlement should be liquidated through our collaborative efforts today to count as a representative American contribution to human freedom and democracy. That the Negro's situation in this hemisphere has this constructive contribution to make to the enlargement of the practice of democracy has been the main conviction and contention of these discussions. All segments of the Negro experience, that of the Latin as well as that of Anglo-Saxon society, must be focused clearly and convincingly if America is to learn effectively the lessons which the Negro's history, achievements and social experience teach. And if the two wings of that experience teach that the open career for talent and the responsibility of the élite for the masses are both necessary for the full solution of the aftermaths of slavery, then the wisdom and uplifting force of both these principles must be effectively joined to enable democracy to rise and soar.

Only so can our whole American society, completely unshackled, fulfill our American institutions of freedom and equality. This, as I see it, is the constructive significance of the Negro to present-day America.

Again I think all those who have so aided and added to the success of this series of lectures, but especially I thank those of you whose collaboration as a patient and responsive audience has given me such needed and welcome help and inspiration. It has been a great pleasure to have been among you and a great privilege to have been able to bring this message. All happiness, progress and prosperity to Haiti. Au revoir!

NOTES

1. Frazier, E. Franklin. 1942. "Some Aspects of Race Relations in Brazil". *Phylon*, 3:3 (1942): 249, 287–295.
2. González Prada, Manuel and Luis Alberto Sánchez Antología, eds. Lima, Peru: Biblioteca Básica del Perú, 1996.
3. The Pan-American prize novel by the Freres Thoby-Marcelin for 1943.

PART II

"Like Rum in the Punch": The Quest for Cultural Democracy

"Like Rum in the Punch": The Quest for Cultural Democracy

I. Critical Pragmatism

If one wants a theoretical justification of the practical engagement of philosophy and philosophers with actual concrete social problems, pragmatism might stand out as an exceptional resource. However, if one wants not just a practical philosophy that has turned away from the problems of philosophers, but one that engages concrete social problems from a philosophical perspective that uses philosophical engagement not as an end in itself but as a tool for social uplift and increased democracy, the bulk of pragmatism is less well-suited to the task. Alain Locke's career is one characterized almost exclusively by practical concern with existential and concrete problems in the life of African descendant peoples. The uncritical reader may often want for more writings by Locke to be expressly and exclusively concerned with traditional philosophical problems, or at least with ostensibly philosophical, even if not novel, concerns. Locke is best understood as a critical pragmatist; one that accepts some of the substantive and methodological tenets of pragmatism while at the same time remaining critical of that philosophical school. Moreover, Locke does not limit himself to a pragmatist philosophical worldview. Locke's philosophy is one heavily informed by philosophical traditions and schools besides pragmatism.

It is worthwhile to consider the reasons for characterizing Locke's philosophy as a form of *critical pragmatism*. That is, one should consider the import of affixing the adjective "critical" to a description of his pragmatism. First, pragmatism is an insufficient label for an accurate characterization of

© The Editor(s) (if applicable) and The Author(s) 2016

J.A. Carter, *African American Contributions to the Americas' Cultures*, DOI 10.1057/978-1-137-56572-3_8

Locke's philosophy. That label alone would align him too closely with the substantive and methodological positions of other pragmatist figures, and in so doing, runs the risk of undervaluing the theoretical departures that he makes from that tradition, and thereby limiting an appreciation of the novelty and uniqueness of his thought. But beyond the potential misunderstanding of Locke's philosophy, there is the possibility of leaving unacknowledged significant and critical aspects of his thinking that transcend the pragmatist tradition. Some of the critical tempers of Locke's philosophy may not be inherent in his overall orientation or any of his substantive commitments; instead, they may come from a comparative understanding of Locke's work in relation to his predecessors, contemporaries, and successors. Their lack of vision, refusal to concern themselves with manifest social problems, blatant racism, sexism, and xenophobia which stand in such stark contrast to his philosophical orientation, may give the impression that he stood closer to pragmatists, and further from African American intellectuals than what a sober analysis of his thought in comparison to theirs may in fact license. The term "critical" is a way of distinguishing Locke from other pragmatists by illuminating his knowledge of, and debt and allegiance to other American traditions of thought, specifically, the philosophizings of Afrodescendant peoples in the USA. This is an area of thought and inquiry of which Locke, unlike many of his pragmatist cohorts, is thoroughly familiar, and which exerted considerable influence on his philosophical worldview. And this is true both in terms of the thinkers with whom he engages, and the subject matter he explores. Indeed, even where Locke's chosen subject matter matched that of other pragmatist philosophers, for example, democracy, value, pluralism, provincialism, art and culture, his reflections on these areas of inquiry differed rather markedly.

Locke's pragmatism is critical for several reasons chief among which is its engagement with concrete social problems from a philosophical perspective—one that frames the issue in terms of the relevant values, principles, rationales, and goals germane to the situation. Second, it is critical owing to its attention to the historical development of social problems, as well as to the success and failure of past attempts at melioration. The primacy of solution implementation over greater theoretical understanding is the third critical aspect of his pragmatism; particularly when the present understanding is sufficient to afford a reasonably straightforward ameliorative program. Critical assessment of the ameliorative program in terms of both its success in addressing the problem, and consequences brought about by the implemented solution for further efforts at realizing a satisfactory state of affairs is the fourth critical aspect. And finally, there is the critique of progress that is often piecemeal and incremental and recognition that recent or past gains may be partially eroded before they are further advanced.

Pragmatism has been challenged from the perspective of critical theory.[1] First, it is alleged that pragmatism is ill-equipped to offer an analysis of structures of power. Second, pragmatism is accused of being the philosophical rationalization of the prevailing ethos in the USA. Third, the anti-foundationalism of pragmatism is seen as an impediment to a proper analysis of power. Finally, pragmatism is accused of failing to produce enlightened individuals aware of their own self-interest in a way that would aid them in avoiding complicity in their own oppression.[2] Locke's pragmatism is able to meet these challenges from a critical perspective, though his is not the perspective of critical theory. Locke's philosophy of race manifests a keen awareness of power relations and structures, in particular, the importance of understanding the connection between racial differentiation, imperial political practice, and domestic systems of political and economic control. Moreover, whereas pragmatism might be understood as a justification for the status quo in the USA, Locke's philosophy is deeply informed by its connection to an intellectual tradition fundamentally at odds with, and thoroughly critical of that society. Finally, Locke's analysis of the impediments to cultural democracy, his naturalized and functional analysis of value, and his advocacy of progressive and cosmopolitan value transformation, all serve to make possible an enlightened self-understanding that open possibilities for Afrodescendant peoples to achieve liberation and enjoy the full exercise of autonomy. These aspects of Locke's philosophy serve to make it a critical pragmatism. Yet, this is not the only way it is unique among pragmatist philosophies. The pluralistic and cosmopolitan dimensions of his thought, along with his philosophical concern with Afrodescendant peoples and expanded notion of democracy, opened the possibility for a broader and more comprehensive, though still characteristically American worldview. This wider orientation is aptly termed Inter-American.

II. THREE INTER-AMERICAN FRAMEWORKS: SLAVERY, RACE, AND DEMOCRACY

For some time now, undoubtedly, we have been aware of great Negro progress in our respective national areas, and have been taking national stock and pride in it. Now however, it seems high time to become more aware of it, as of other aspects of our American life, in an inter-American perspective.

Though needing, let us hope, no such extreme conversion today, the intelligent and forward thinking public of the Americas needs reinforcing evidence of the present cultural attainments and growing cultural influence of the American Negro. It must come, too, with that overwhelming effect that can only derive from corroborative evidence from every quarter and from every one of the American nations having any considerable Negro contingent. Certainly such evidence is rapidly coming in, and it seems to reflect only our naturally limited information if such cultural progress seems to be more developed in North or South or Mid-America. Someday, and as soon as possible, it is to be hoped the general record will be compiled in its hemispheric rather than just a narrow nationalistic scope. Someday, too, and as soon after the conclusion of the war as possible, it is also hoped that inter-American exhibits and visits will make wider known and reciprocally appreciated the contemporary personalities and contributions of this cultural advance of the various contingents of American Negro life.[3]

Any attempt at articulating a coherent view of the Americas, attributable to Locke, that extends beyond the limited province of the USA requires one to take a bit of intellectual license. Locke did not write much directly on the commonalities and variances between the myriad American cultures. This creates a situation in which contemporary scholars of Locke's work must exercise some creativity in coming to an understanding of his likely views on the subject. The task is not simply to elucidate Locke's own considered and stated views on the subject; so much as an innovative exegesis which draws on multiple aspects of his overall thought on a plurality of subjects. Potential rewards are proportionate to the challenge of such an endeavor if it is able to yield a clear articulation of a position, consistent, at the very least, but perhaps, it is to be hoped, even implied, with some non-negligible degree of force by his comprehensive philosophic worldview. Conceptual resources pertinent to matters of contemporary concern can be found as readily in pondering over what prior intellectuals neglected to say, and accounting for the seeming dereliction, as in concerning ourselves with what they did say.

The Americas are a region that not only shares common historical threads but also diverges at important and interesting points. Chief among Locke's philosophical insights on this matter is his recognition that focusing on North America resulted in at best a myopic view of all of the Americas, or at worst a complete blindness to large portions of the Americas. On this particular point, his contribution is most pioneering, representing as it does, a nearly six-decade advance on current pragmatist and American philosophical scholarship. Only recently have pragmatists—coming mostly from recent members of that philosophic tradition closely associated with Latin American philosophy—begun to pay attention to the idea of the Americas as interconnected and interdependent regions also marked by diverse and divergent histories.

Thinking comprehensively and programmatically about the Americas is not an attempt to establish an artificial unity across the continent. Rather, the aim is to pursue the possibility of discovering cultural cognates that resonate with the plurality of cultures which comprise the Americas. Locke's own approach to theorizing the Americas in this work is mediated through the experiences of those of African heritage in various American contexts. An approach which, incidentally (though perhaps purposefully) evidences the variety of Afrodescendant populations to be found in the Americas; all the while serving as a coordinating thread with which to weave together into an, at least coherent, if not homogenous whole, ostensibly disparate strands of African American life. Through this African American lens, one is able to see the larger effects of historical and social processes, even as they are varied to fit specific contexts, across time and place.

One of the defining features of the lectures presented in this volume is the demonstration by Locke of an incipient Inter-American philosophical methodology. This methodology centers around the philosophical exploration of a phenomenon, concept, or problem that is ubiquitous throughout the Americas as a means of understanding the resonances and deviations of different American cultures in regard to that phenomenon, concept or problem. So that what one finds in these lectures is the use of the phenomenon of slavery, specifically, the African Slave trade, the concept of race, the Negro race in particular, and the problem of democracy as methodological points of departure from which to philosophize about the Americas. To be sure, no one of these approaches is all-encompassing, as each likely fails to capture some important aspect of some portion of the Americas worthy of theoretical reflection. Neither are these lines of investigation mutually exclusive. In fact, Locke's own approach is not to pursue them independently; rather, he manages to weave them together in a complimentary fashion. He writes early in the first lecture:

> I am sanguine about the purpose and propriety of my mission, particularly in view of the double bond of sympathy and interest between us; for we have, have we not, both the fellowship of democracy and that of the confraternity of race. Indeed, I scarcely know which of the two to emphasize, facing the

agreeable alternative of saluting you either as fellow-Americans, in the best and generic sense of that term, or as comrades of race. Small matter, however, for it is my eventual purpose to tie the two together, having chosen as my general subject: The Negro's Contribution to the Culture of the Americas. In this way I hope to be able to make North American culture a little better understood and appreciated, and especially that part of it which has been vitally influenced by the American Negro. Also, though I hasten to confess myself less competent in this field, it is my purpose to show how importantly and strategically this Negro and originally African segment of culture exists as a common denominator, little known but quite historic and fundamental, between some of the most important national cultures of the Americas.[4]

Locke begins the inaugural lecture by announcing that "[t]he new order of the new day in human relations is reciprocity, not aggression, mutual assistance not overlordship, fraternity, in short, not paternalism."[5] Locke sees his participation in the professorial exchange as a form of cultural reciprocity. Locke confesses that he has two favorable choices of addressing his audience as fellow democratic citizens of the Americas, or as racial comrades. He proposes, however, to bring the two together through his chosen theme for the lectures that is: The Negro's Contribution to the Culture of the Americas. One hope that he expresses early on is to help make North American culture better known in other parts of the Americas, in particular, those aspects of it that have been most influenced by African descendant peoples. In regard to the latter, he aims to demonstrate the important and strategic place that original African cultural elements and distinctively Negro elements occupy as a common denominator between a variety of American national cultures. These represent historic and fundamental aspects of many American national cultures Locke claims, even if they are little known. Throughout North, South, and Central America and the Caribbean the various arts have been enlivened and revitalized by Negro idioms, traditions, and artistic and cultural products. Locke hopes that our mutual debt can serve as the foundation of "an important new spiritual dimension into our Inter-American unity, and help develop among and between us the full potential of social and cultural democracy."[6]

A.   An Inter-American Philosophy of Slavery

The first Inter-American framework to consider is slavery, that historical phenomenon responsible for bringing large populations of African descendant peoples to the Americas even before they were fully racialized as Negro. As Locke understands it, the enslavement of African descendant peoples in the Americas is a phenomenon that is inextricably related to the development of theories of race and the evolution of American democracy on the continent. Slavery has had far-reaching effects throughout the Americas even as the particular shape of these effects has varied across different regions. The plurality of America's cultures, its racial creeds and practices, the contacts and interrelations between races, the development of its democratic institutions and forms all require an understanding of its slave history, both in terms of an understanding of which populations were brought from Africa to which parts of the Americas, and the ways in which enslaved populations were able to exert an influence in the emerging New World civilization being forcibly imposed on existing indigenous populations. Locke notes the significance of the Atlantic slave trade to an interrelated understanding of the Americas when he writes:

> Slavery is one of the oldest human institutions, nearly as old as man and nearly as universal. But the longest, the most extensive and the most cruel chapter in the history of human slavery is that dark African chapter of the trans-Atlantic slave trade precipitated by the colonial settlement of the Americas. We must never forget how substantially it helped to make the colonial conquest of the New World possible, thus laying the foundation of that American civilization which we all enjoy today. The slave trade involved the Three Americas. It has affected permanently both the population and the culture of the Americas; especially Mid-America. It has influenced the life of the Americas both for good and evil, and almost everywhere in America, to one degree or another, the shadow of slavery's yet incomplete undoing still clouds the possibilities of a fully democratic American society.[7]

As an organizing framework for philosophical reflection, the Trans-Atlantic trade obviates the necessity of thinking beyond the narrow parameters of how it unfolded in any one region of the Americas and invited a more systematic inquiry into its more general effects, and its relation to trans-global phenomena such as colonization and white supremacy. The prescient insight that Locke offers to Inter-American philosophy is the notion that it should not be limited to merely juxtaposing American philosophical traditions, nor to merely presenting together, but as unrelated, the ways different traditions have approached the same subject. Rather, Inter-American philosophy stands to offer more and deeper knowledge if it can meld into a more comprehensive philosophical orientation the multiplicity of philosophical points of view to be found in the Americas. This is not to suggest that there is, or can be, complete agreement and coherence between all such philosophical traditions, that may be neither possible nor desirable. But Locke's approach exemplifies in the case of slavery that more than reconciling philosophical perspectives these perspectives can be brought into a meaningful discourse by attending to the way that each informs our understanding of a phenomenon present throughout the Americas. Then it is not an issue, for example, of reconciling pragmatism in North America with positivism in Latin America, or Marxism in the Caribbean with Continental philosophy in Brazil. Instead, the task of Inter-American philosophy becomes an investigation into the way that each of these perspectives offers insights into issues of paramount concern to many segments of different American nations, and the ways that knowledge can be furthered by tending to the work of multiple philosophical schools operative in the Americas.

> In so doing slavery did two peculiar and significant things which have determined the course of American history and influenced the character of American civilization: first, American Slavery, since it was of the domestic variety, planted the Negro in the very core of the dominant white civilization, permitting not only its rapid assimilation by the Negro but its being, in turn, deeply and continuously counter-influenced culturally by the Negro; and second, it also planted the Negro—and that holds true for today as well as for the past, at the moral and political core of a basically democratic society, so that around him and his condition wherever there are undemocratic inconsistencies, must center the whole society's struggle for the full and continuous development of freedom.[8]

There are several benefits that accrue to any serious and sustained attempt at philosophizing in an Inter-American context—even when that exploration is circumscribed by the domain of a specific historical phenomenon or a single racial group—not least of which is the potential for increased cross-cultural understanding. Insofar as the Americas are comprised of multifarious cultures, a broader philosophical framework can serve, not only to bring out the relative distinctiveness of each of these cultures but their formal and substantive similarities as well. Viewed in comparative relation to one another, and in a manner consistent with Locke's relativist position,[9] the various cultures of the Americas would all become better understood by persons internal and external to each of those cultures, to whatever extent a comparative and functional understanding of the values of each of those cultures makes that possible. With regard to the more circumspect project of looking at the American portions of the African diaspora, this larger framework obviates a more heterogeneous, and thereby accurate picture of African American life, and the variety of forms of living, ethnic variation, religious practice, and artistic expression to be found among Afrodescendant peoples. As an ethnoracial group, African descendant peoples are spread across national, cultural, and ethnic boundaries. It is for this reason that a comprehensive view is theoretically enlightening. In looking at the varied existence of communities of African descended peoples in the Americas, as well as the myriad responses to their existence in different contexts one has an effective entry point for an examination of a more wide-ranging set of phenomena than Afrodescendant peoples as a social race. An intercontinental perspective promises to increase both the breadth and the depth of our understanding of world historical processes and agents.

B.   An Inter-American Philosophy of Race

The second point of departure is ethnic race, which Locke uses as a framework for the Inter-American inquiry he conducts over the course of the six lectures. Race, much like slavery, is for Locke an organizing principle that positions him to engage with myriad aspects of the Americas simultaneously. Free from the tendency in the USA to see race as binary, Locke is able to revise his conception of a race so that it can account for the variegated race creeds and practices of different regions of the Americas. Methodologically, the focus on a specific ethnoracial category, which Locke simply terms Negro, serves as a common starting point for philosophical inquiry in multiple regions of the Americas. Locke writes:

> In the first place, in every one of the countries where he constitutes a considerable proportion of the population, the Negro represents a conspicuous index by which the practical efficiency and integrity of that particular country's democracy can readily be gauged and judged. For the same high visibility which internally makes possible ready discrimination against Negroes makes the domestic practices of race externally all the more conspicuous and observable in the enlarging spotlight of international relations. However fundamental the domestic issues of race may be, today and for the future we must all be particularly concerned about their international consequences. This holds in general on a world scale (see note 9).

Here again, we see the way in which Locke's chosen focal points for his Inter-American investigation combine in interesting ways. Not only does the ethnoracial population of African descendant peoples provide an entry point into a number of significant American regions, it also serves as a springboard into important areas of inquiry in the Americas that extend well beyond any particular ethnoracial group, and even beyond the category of race.

> Here the American treatment of the Negro can have and already has had serious repercussions on enlightened Asiatic and African public opinion and confidence. Or, for that matter, so will our treatment of any racial minority such as the treatment of American segments of the Hindu or the Chinese resident among us. But this situation holds with intensified force as between the Americas and with particular reference to the widely distributed American groups of Negro and mixed Negro descent. For historical and inescapable reasons, the Negro has thus become a basic part and conspicuous symbol of the cause of democracy in our Western hemisphere.[10]

Admittedly, one may wonder why Locke is uniquely suited to do this conceptual work. How, a critic might ask, does Locke specifically help to advance the project of philosophizing about the Americas in terms of their interrelations, especially given the particularly glaring limitations and omissions of his approach; namely, the almost total exclusion of indigenous peoples in his account of the Americas? The worry is also relevant to the Inter-American point of view with which Locke begins; namely, slavery, as the African slave trade grew significantly as a result of failed attempts at enslaving indigenous populations in the Americas, and the racial constitution of many contemporary Latin American countries has been determined in large part by which groups were successfully enslaved in various parts of the Americas.

By way of reply to these concerns it is important to note that while he does not address them explicitly or fully, Locke is not unaware of the widespread influence and contribution of indigenous civilizations and cultures to American cultures and civilization. Though it is not his chosen topic for the lectures, Locke demonstrates this awareness when he writes in the inaugural lecture:

> Already under its influence, in the United States, and still more deliberately in Mexico, the culture of the American Indian is being completely revalued. It is no longer being regarded as a despised and isolated folk culture, alien to that of the educated elite, but rather as something which, in addition to being a precious heritage of those who are its direct descendants, has contributed to the general culture, and has possibilities, when properly appreciated and developed, of making further contributions. The same is true of the enlightened contemporary view of the Negro's folk culture in North America, and the parallel movement for a higher evaluation of

the Afro-Cuban, the Afro-Brazilian, and the Afro-Antillean factors in their respective regional cultures is part of the same tendency.[11]

Moreover, his overall account of ethnic race (as will be seen more fully below) holds that social races are almost always composite entities. Locke claims that thinking in the Americas has retained an undesirable colonial trait; namely, identifying nationality with culture, and far too often that of the dominant culture group. The problem Locke sees is that this represents a failure to accurately understand the reality of most American nations, "[f]or the typical American state, whether North or South American," he claims "is both multi-racial and multi-national in its human and cultural composition."[12] Also, it should be borne in mind that while Locke's focus is on a specific race, that ought not to be taken to indicate that he does not think that similar studies could be conducted through the medium of different racial populations that exist in the Americas. One should not assume from Locke's focus on a specific ethnoracial group (or particular historical phenomenon) that the underlying Inter-American methodology must always attach to that particular group (or phenomenon). At the same time that Locke aims to broaden his perspective he means to remain focused on concrete experiential realities. In therms of the phenomenon or objects that the Inter-American orientation brings into philosophical view, Locke, in keeping with his axiological thinking, finds the particular objects and phenomena to be highly interchangeable. An important upshot of his position is that even a focus on a specific ethnic race in the Americas involves attending to the other racial populations which it has influenced and which have had an influence on the racial population in question. In point of fact, Locke's understanding of African descendant populations in the Americas seeks to understand them in the context of their reciprocal relations with other social races, and the way that Afrodescendant populations themselves are fundamentally hybrid formations of various ethnic races present in the Americas. Especially, is this recognition necessitated by the realities of racial formation throughout Latin America and the Caribbean.

C.   An Inter-American Philosophy of Democracy

The third Inter-American framework is a concept that Locke terms cultural democracy. More than a concern for the particular forms of governance employed in American nations, cultural democracy is meant to capture a social arrangement in which a plurality of people is able to cooperate on equal standing. Locke was stridently committed to the belief that "[t]he parity of nations, races and cultures is … the next and necessary step in the evolution of the democratic ideal."[13] Such commitment necessitated a re-evaluation of American values. Specifically, a commitment to equality and fraternity requires that one jettison or transform the provincialisms that are often deeply embedded in our group associations. Parochialism about race, nationality, and culture unnecessarily limits our self-conceptions. But Locke seems not to think mere tolerance is enough. Beyond that, a plu-ralistic spirit that values, embraces and promotes diversity is needed to advance continued and just group relations. There are various impedi-ments to the realization of cultural democracy, according to Locke, chief among them are parochialism, provincialism, and racial chauvinism. Nearly all American nations, because of their ethnoracial diversity must devise strategies for overcoming these obstacles, and therein lies its poten-tial as an Inter-American philosophical framework. Our understanding of democracy in relation to culture throughout the Americas is broadened and made more critically accurate through reflection on the concept from the vantage point of various American cultures and nations.

Cultural hybridity and cross-cultural fertilization, Locke notes, are far more frequent and fecund than has been recognized. Foreign soils have nurtured some of the most fascinating cultural products; elements that faired far better in new environments than in their native lands. Often, it is from the lower poorer classes, not infrequently immigrants or forced transplants, that idiomatic transformations in the arts, dance, music, and folklore are spurred. Moreover, it seems that a substantial portion of the most highly regarded aspects of culture is the result of cultural hybrid-ity and cross-cultural exchange. All throughout the Americas, wherever Afrodescendant populations, whether amid Anglo-Saxon or Latin cultural elements, has existed in considerable numbers, their cultural products have exhibited these truths. In the Americas, Locke sees, many exam-ples of oppressed peoples, specifically, African descendant and indigenous communities supplying the dominant spiritual influences on national cul-tures. The American tradition of coloniality has obfuscated the important democratic lesson in such phenomena, but the lesson is nonetheless there to be learned. Locke opines that "[w]e might even go so far as to say that our culture had been more democratic than we ourselves have been."[14]

All American societies through the comprehension of such ideas stand to learn an important lesson about democracy. The outmoded aristocratic notion of higher and lower culture, stratified according to social tradition is giving way to an increasingly democratic understanding of cultural exchanges between groups. The relative value of a culture is to be determined by the significance and impact in particular circumstances of its creative role in the larger society. Here Locke believes that Afrodescendant people in North America are an instructive case in point. Because African Americans were made to adopt the language and religion of the majority culture, they were less socially distant from that culture than perhaps African descendant peoples were in other parts of the Americas. Despite the social distance that existed and the social, political, legal, and economic disadvantages of African Americans they nonetheless had a strong counter-influence on North American culture. Despite being hindered in formal culture, many characteristic, expressive, and idiomatic qualities of the Negro's racial tradition has left a lasting and far-reaching imprint on the larger USA culture. African descendant people's role in the creation of a uniquely American music was already widely acknowledged, but the same imprint is to be found in other cultural fields including art, dance, drama, literature, and folklore. One expressed purpose of the lecture series is to detail this cultural role and contribution on the part of the Negro. Of primary concern when Locke makes this observation in the first lecture, is to illuminate the underlying principle that cultural influence is often reciprocal even between relatively powerful majority groups, and comparatively powerless minority groups, and provide an example of "a handicapped minority becoming culturally influential despite such handicaps."[15] Locke acknowledges that it may seem paradoxical to some that the folk-life and folk-spirit of African Americans as a subjugated group could have a substantial impact on some of the most characteristic aspects of American culture. He explains away the seeming paradox by claiming that there is a sufficiently deep and universal reason for the influence. It is because "even in being characteristically racial, these creative expressions have also been basically and universally human, and have thus obtained a contagious and "irresistible hold upon human sympathy and understanding.""[16] By way of concrete illustration, Locke looks to the "Spirituals" as an illustrative example of the paradox. The spirituals are paragons of African American creative musical expression in the USA while being at the same time identifiably racial and recognizably universal and human, and characteristically representative of North American culture.

D.   The Future Prospects of Inter-American Philosophy

Inter-American philosophy is a way of overcoming a philosophical provincialism that is Locke's immediate concern. Philosophical provincialism seeks to identify certain concerns, thinkers and philosophers, and specific philosophizings as the exclusive purview of a given philosophical tradition. It takes philosophical traditions as having a unique right or privileged access to particular inquiries or forms of investigation. Even where provincial philosophies are somewhat expansive, they are able to set the criteria for inclusion in the tradition and often do so in ways that privilege a given approach, particular theorists or concerns to the exclusion of philosophical traditions that diverge too significantly from the recognized and favored form of philosophizing they endorse. This is seen, for example, in attempts to articulate and argue for a broader understanding of pragmatism throughout the Americas. This, to be sure, is one approach to Inter-American philosophy, and not an obviously bankrupt one. But it runs the danger of setting up an unnecessary and ultimately counter-productive hierarchy between American philosophical traditions as it inevitably entails a decision about which iterations of, for example, Latin American or Caribbean traditions count as "pragmatist" and which do not, and makes either fidelity to supposedly central tenets of pragmatism or commensurability with the philosophies of its canonical figures a requisite for inclusion in the expanded notion of pragmatism and a legitimating criterion for pragmatist philosophers to take other American philosophical traditions seriously.

An Inter-American philosophical approach has the potential to deepen the philosophical enterprise by exposing the arguments and positions of philosophers to myriad critical perspectives. In much the same way that the scientific enterprise is benefitted by the plurality of competent inquirers investigating similar phenomena and engaging in an evaluation of the investigatory methods of other inquirers; so too, does a theoretical point of view that extends beyond the specious claim(s) to universality of Anglo-American philosophy, and escapes the narrow confines of ethnically or racially delimited American philosophies hold out the possibility for a more accurate, nuanced, critical and productively engaging philosophical orientation. An environment in which persons are regularly brought into theoretical and practical contact with critical perspectives of groups of which they are not members—provided they are oriented toward such difference in a manner that makes them receptive to it—is one that holds out the possibility of greater—perhaps ever-increasing provided the necessary orientation is maintained over time—objectivity that is the aim of knowledge. The practical realization of the sort of approach Locke undertakes in the lectures provides a noteworthy example against the dereliction of many of his contemporary American and pragmatist philosophers, and much needed source material for present-day American philosophers to think more comprehensively and simultaneously conceive of American philosophy in broader and more nuanced ways.

There are of course practical advantages that emanate from a more expansive view of the Americas, principal among which is the fact that knowledge of the efforts of others at meliorating similar problems in different contexts can strengthen one's own resolve and resources for solving problems. Especially as we come to greater realization of the multiplicity of successful adaptive responses by different ethnic, racial, and cultural groups in the Americas to global and historical forces that bear on them all in varying degrees, do these groups stand to gain the wisdom of not only their own but of other's experiences. Furthermore, there is historical precedence to support not only the interconnectedness but also the theoretical salience of scholarship generated in one part of the Americas being applicable to other American contexts. Liberation theology, for example, was largely a Latin American invention that sought at least in part to address issues of social justice germane to Latin America but was appropriated by African American theologians in their own struggles for social justice. Couple with that the far-reaching influence of theorists such as Frantz Fanon, W.E.B. Du Bois, and Amié Césaire, and their particular appositeness to the issues facing African descended peoples in the Americas, and one gains a clearer sense of the propriety of theorizing the Americas as interrelated.

Moreover, it is hoped that a focus on all of the Americas and their interrelation will help to see beyond the superficial isolation of American cultures and the artificial divisions across culture groups. For instance, the lives of many Latin and North American cultures interact rather closely and in antagonistic ways. The broader philosophic perspective that Locke advocates can provide a framework from which to consider these issues without arbitrarily privileging any one perspective—presumably philosophic theory will not countenance the sort of biased perspectives that all too often characterizes political discourse on the subject. One might worry that Locke may not be useful for addressing present concerns, but insofar as one seeks to rest such efforts on sound theoretical justifications, Locke is an indispensable resource for many reasons, not least of which is the fact that his own efforts at constructing sound theory are rooted in praxis aimed at the amelioration of concrete social problems of his day as they pertain not only to North American Negro populations, but Southern and Caribbean as well. We must be careful in our assessment of what exactly it is we are asking a theorist such as Locke in this situation to do. It would be absurd to expect him to be able to solve either the practical or theoretical issues of contemporary concern where those are more than the mere persistence of problems of their own day. What instead Locke has to offer is a stable point of departure in the form of a philosophical springboard from which to launch or own ameliorative efforts, as well as a sound philosophical framework suited to facilitate a proper determination of the nature of a given social problem and the likely prospects for its successful resolution. Beyond this, Locke offers further an instructive example of the kind of critical analysis and insight requisite for potentially ameliorative social and cultural criticism. The example stands out all the more when viewed against the relative blindness of some of his contemporaries to issues of which he was keenly aware. As has been argued earlier, such dimensions of Locke's thought are what set him apart as a critical pragmatist, or perhaps better, a critical Inter-American pragmatist philosopher.

III.   African American Contributions
in the Americas: Race, Culture, Art, and Literature

I have often thought that the greatest obstacle that has prevented the world realizing unity has been a false conception of what unity itself meant in this case. It is a notion, especially characteristic of the West, that to be one effectively, we must all be alike and that to be at peace, we must all have the same interests. On the contrary, apart from the practical impossibility of such a form, and its stagnant undesirability, we have, in the very attempt to impose it, the greatest disruptive force active in the modern world today.[17]

The purpose of this section is to explore the fundamental idea of the lectures themselves; namely, the contribution of Afrodescendant peoples to the cultures of the Americas. This rather complex idea is analyzed into its constituent elements in order to come to a clear understanding of what exactly Locke thinks is involved in the larger idea. The constituent concepts of this larger idea are race, culture and the paired notion of what it means to make a contribution to culture. In the final analysis, these three concepts are brought together to gain an understanding of what Locke means by making a racial contribution to culture, before moving on in subsequent sections to a consideration of what exactly the cultural contribution of the Negro has been.

A. Locke's Conception of Race

The concept of race is an important aspect of Locke's overall philosophy, and as was seen earlier a crucial framework for his Inter-American methodology in addition to being one of the chosen topics for the lectures. Locke's theory of race draws a distinction between three primary conceptions of race: anthropological, political and social. Anthropological conceptions of race explain racial differentiation in terms of supposedly biological or ethnological features of human populations. Racial differentiation, on such accounts, is a matter of historical or natural deviation between human populations. Political conceptions of race, on Locke's view, are based on successful or unsuccessful interracial contacts which leave social groups in comparatively dominant or subordinate positions. Racial differentiation is the result of the exercise or lack of political power on this account. Finally, according to Locke, social conceptions of race account for racial differentiation in terms of uniquely characteristic cultural traits, lifestyles, and forms of expression. Racial differentiation, on this account, is the byproduct of subcultural inflection.[18]

Race and culture, according to Locke, are both widely thought to be important to the scientific study of man and society, yet with regard to both, there is relatively little in the way of agreement as to their meanings. Locke's philosophy of race offers "an examination of their supposed relationship one to the other" as he finds that the mistaken assumption of a fixed relationship between race and culture has been the cause of much difficulty and confusion on the subject.[19] As to the relationship of race to culture, Locke writes:

> It will be our contention that far from being constants, these important aspects of human society are variables, and in the majority of instances not even paired variables, and that though they have at all times significant and definite relationships, they nevertheless are in no determinate way organically or causally related. And if this should be so, whole masses of elaborately constructed social theory and cultural philosophizing fall with the destruction of a common basic assumption, that has been taken as a common foundation for otherwise highly divergent and even antagonistic theorizing.[20]

Locke agrees that race and culture are important aspects of human society and, by implication, important concepts in a scientific understanding of man and society. This is prima facie incompatible with eliminativism about race and for that reason a somewhat paradoxical aspect of Locke's view, which on the whole has some rather remarkable affinities with racial eliminativist positions. Locke denies that race and culture are constants: that is, they are not fixed units of social or anthropological analysis. Perhaps he means to deny that race or culture remain fixed over time, and across geographic locations. He positively asserts that they are variables, indicating that they are not fixed points of analysis, and are subject to change over time, and in different places. Locke denies further that they co-vary. Variations in race need not be linked to variations in culture, nor vice versa.

Immediately after the above claim which in effect severs the link between race and culture, Locke asserts that they are "at all times" in "significant and definite relationships"[21] with each other. The claim that the relationships between race and culture are significant indicates that they bear some importance to the study of man and society; the relationships are not trivial. Locke's claim that the relationships are definite indicates that they are in large part observable, and perhaps measureable, and that race and culture are not completely independent of each other. However, Locke subsequently rejects the idea that they are in any "determinate way organically or causally connected."[22] The idea is that though race and culture will frequently bear some relationship to each other, those relationships are not necessary, nor are they clearly, or in a specifiable way, organic or causal.

One way to think about the relationships not being necessary is to consider that for any given non-trivial relationship that exists between a race and a culture that relationship need not exist between another race and culture. As for the relationships being determinately organic or causal, there are two possible interpretations of what Locke might mean. One interpretation is that race and culture are not organically or causally related, that no relationship that it would make sense to describe in either of these two ways exists between race and culture. The second interpretation is that race and culture may be causally or organically related, but that such relations between them are not determinate. The relations may fail to be determinate in that they are not settled or fixed between a given race and culture, or that they are not set or stable between all races and cultures. This way of understanding Locke suggests that there can be organic or causal relationships between races and cultures, but that such relations are not necessary, and even where they do obtain they are not hard and fast. Locke writes:

> This position, differing from that of the school of interpretation which denies all significant connection between racial and cultural factors, does not deny that race stands for significant social characters and culture-traits or represents in given historical contexts characteristic differentiations of culture-type. However, it does insist against the assumption of any such constancy, historical or intrinsic, as would make it possible to posit an organic connection between them and to argue on such grounds the determination of one by the other.[23]

Locke further claims that "[i]n some revised and reconstructed form we may anticipate the continued even if restricted use of these terms as more or less necessary and basic concepts that cannot be eliminated altogether."[24] However, he continues, to state that the concept of race "must nevertheless be so safe-guarded in this continued use as not to give further currency to the invalidated assumptions concerning them."[25] This appears to pit Locke against racial eliminativism. Though it should be noted here that he is making the claim about both terms, not one or the other. Locke seems to be claiming that we can no more sensibly or reasonably eliminate "race" than we can "culture." His claim is limited in some important ways. First, it applies to a "revised or reconstructed" concept of race, presumably, a revision that corrects the mistaken belief that race determines culture or cultural aptitude in a fixed and determinate relationship to culture. Locke admits that the continued use of the terms would likely be restricted, and he claims that as they are "more or less necessary and basic" concepts to the study of man and society they cannot be "eliminated altogether."[26] There is then the possibility of a partial elimination. Locke places restrictions or criteria on possible revisions of the concepts. The revision must be done carefully enough to avoid giving further currency to invalidated conceptions concerning them. That is, the revised or reconstructed concepts face an epistemological hurdle; they must not countenance false beliefs.

Locke attributes the notion that race is a determining factor in culture to Arthur de Gobineau, though he claims its scientific justification comes primarily from the social evolutionary theory of Herbert Spencer.[27] The notion of a fixed relationship between race and culture was used primarily to justify the social evolutionist belief in a series of historical stages in progressive social development. The notion of a fixed linkage between race and culture has been the analogue in social theory to the concept of heredity in biology. The stock notions of race capacity and racial heredity have similarly gone through a process of acceptance, rejection, and revision.[28] Locke asserts that several lines of argument have disproved the false notion that race and culture stand in a fixed relationship along with the mistaken belief that they justify a "supposedly universal process of development."[29]

Locke was optimistic that more objective analysis of culture into social races—a series of relatively divergent and basic culture-types—would result in an understanding of their development or evolution that yields "a standard of value for relative culture grading."[30] Cultures, for Locke, are best treated as specific and highly composite, and ethnicities, as the particular outcome of specific social histories. Locke clarifies what he means by "this reversal of emphasis," between race and culture; namely, "that instead of the race explaining the cultural condition, the cultural conditions must explain the race traits."[31] Moreover, "instead of artificially extracted units representing race types," Locke contends that "the newer scientific approach demands that we deal with concrete culture-types which as often as not are composite racially speaking, and have only an artificial ethnic unity of historical derivation and manufacture."[32] Locke's claim that race is, in reality, an "artificial ethnic unity" reads as a kind of antirealism about race or ethnicity.[33] The phrase "historical derivation and manufacture" certainly indicates that ethnicities or ethnic unity is a constructed phenomenon for Locke, but that need not make them unreal. Artifacts can be real things, but need not be, and they are often not naturally occurring. The word "artificial" is ambiguous as to the reality of ethnic unity. Having come to what he thinks is "the correct scientific understanding of culture;" namely, that it is highly composite, and produced and participated in by a large variety of human beings, Locke raises the question of whether or not that precludes the possibility of any serious consideration of race in connection with culture. Foreshadowing his positive account, Locke writes, "[s]o considerable is the shift of emphasis and meaning that at times it does seem that the best procedure would be to substitute for the term race the term culture-group."[34]

The important thing to take away from this observation according to Locke is that we need not "deny the existence of these characteristic racial molds" in denying that they are hereditary biological or psychological traits.[35] Locke suspects that a more tenable doctrine of the relationship of race and culture would have emerged if more attention had been paid to the ethnic; rather than, anthropological characters of populations. If this had been done, Locke speculates, race would likely have been understood to be socially inherited and racial "distinctions due to the selective psychological "set" of established cultural reactions."[36] Here Locke's view of race is an importantly "learned" or epistemic mode of being: something that persons not only acquire through a process of enculturation or socialization but once acquired conditions the way one perceives and understands the world. He writes:

> The best consensus of opinion seems to be that race is a fact in the social or ethnic sense, that it has been very erroneously associated with race in the physical sense and is therefore not scientifically commensurate with factors or conditions which explain or have produced physical race characters and differentiations, that it has a vital and significant relation to social culture, and that it must be explained in terms of social and historical causes such as have caused similar differentiations of culture-type as pertain in lesser degree between nations, tribes, classes, and even family strains.[37]

The claim that race is a fact in the social or ethnic sense seems to align Locke's view with the contemporary constructionist accounts of race. Moreover, the observation that social or ethnic race has been erroneously associated with physical race, suggests that Locke would share with many contemporary constructionist accounts of race the belief that races are not biologically distinct populations; race for Locke is a social, and not a biological, reality. It is significantly related to social culture. Races are determined or differentiated by social and historical forces of the same sort that cause differences in culture-type between nations and classes. Locke continues, "[m]ost authorities are now reconciled to two things,—first, the necessity of a thorough-going redefinition of the nature of race, and second, the independent definition of race in the ethnic or social sense together with the independent investigation of its differences and their causes apart from the investigation of the factors and differentiae of physical race."[38]

B.   The Concept of Ethnic Race

On Locke's account, two distinct conceptions of race emerge: one, anthropological or biological race, the other, social or ethnic race. The latter, he claims is the more useful in explaining cultural assimilation, as the former has been thoroughly undermined as the cause of cultural variation. Moreover, the distinctions made, the very populations constituted by, anthropological race, rarely if ever coincide with those of ethnic race. The two conceptions carve up the world differently and, of the two, Locke finds ethnic race the more scientifically tenable and useful. Instead of regarding culture "as expressive of race," Locke's view understands "race … as itself a culture product."[39] Locke states that "[r]ace in the vital and basic sense is simply and primarily the culture-heredity, and that in its blendings and differentiations is properly analyzed on the basis of conformity to or variance from culture-type"[40] Locke further states that "culture-type or social race is the important fact and concept" for understanding cultural assimilation.[41]

Locke denies that his conception of the relationship of race to culture is a form of extreme relativism. Having clarified what his view is not meant to claim and contrasting it with other views, Locke begins his presentation of his positive view of the relation of race to culture. He begins by pointing out that there is

> an open question as to the association of certain ethnic groups with definite culture-traits and culture types under circumstances where there is evidently a greater persistence of certain strains and characteristics in their culture than of other factors. The stability of such factors and their resistance to direct historical modification marks out the province of that aspect of the problem of race which is distinctly ethnological and which the revised notion of ethnic race must cover.[42]

In circumstances where certain strains and characteristics are more persistent in the cultures of certain ethnic groups than they are in others, Locke contends, there is an open question as to the association of those specific culture-traits and culture-types with those ethnicities. The relative stability and resiliency of such factors to historical modification demarcates the distinctively ethnological dimension of the problem of race. The revised concept of ethnic race is meant to cover this distinctly ethnological aspect of the problem of race.[43] Locke held that race was in point of fact a social and cultural category rather than a biological one. For this reason, he developed the notion of ethnic race or culture group. By ethnic race, I take Locke to mean a peculiar set of psychological and affective responsive dispositions, expressed or manifested as cultural traits, socially inherited and able to be attributed through historical contextualization to a specifiable group of people. The concept of ethnic race is a way of preserving the demonstrated distinctiveness of various groupings of human beings in terms of characteristic traits, lifestyles, forms of expression; without resulting to the scientifically invalidated notion of biological race. Locke acknowledges that there is no anthropological explanation to be given for the seemingly stable and stock character of certain ethnic traits; this is why he supposes that they are best interpreted as ethnically characteristic. These ethnic traits are far from absolute or permanent, and neither is there sufficient psychological evidence to construe them as inherent.[44] Yet, they seem to be integrally connected in ways that are not sufficiently explained by historical combinations. Locke further comments that it is difficult to find common historical causes that account for the "relative constancy" of these ethnic traits.[45]

Ethnic race captures better the myriad differences in social, cultural, and historical conditions that constitute various culture groups without the scientifically indefensible reliance on biological factors. Race is no longer, on this view, thought to be the progenitor of culture; instead, race in the social and ethnic sense is understood to be a concrete culture-type; the result of subcultural variation. A more scientific understanding of man replaces the abstract artifice of biological race, and requires that we deal with concrete culture-types which are frequently complex amalgamations of supposed races united principally by entrenchment of customary reactions, standardized practices, traditional forms of expression and interaction, in sum, the specific history of a given people in a particular place. What race amounts to for Locke is the characteristic differentiation of culture-type perpetuated through social heredity. In other words, race is a matter of distinctive variations within culture transmitted across generations. Locke's notion of ethnic race raises a number of questions: For one this would mean that there are far more races on the planet than previously thought. In fact, many of the groups putatively regarded as one race will be found on this account to constitute several different races. It is noteworthy and perhaps illuminating of Locke's conception of ethnic or social race that the groupings of human persons formerly thought to constitute "races" in the biological sense such as "Negro," "Caucasian," or "Asian" are in fact each composed of several different social or ethnic races. In Locke's view, there are many so-called Negro, "Caucasian," or "Asian" races. While the notion of race has been invalidated as an explanation of culture groups understood as totalities, Locke quickly notes, race does help to explain various cultural components within a given culture.

By way of illustration of Locke's point here consider African Americans in the United States. In Locke's view they share a common culture with white Americans in terms of language, religion, aesthetic sense and many other cultural elements. However, even in having these things in common there are characteristic, qualitatively distinct, and phenomenologically unique forms that common language, religion, and aesthetic sense takes among and between African Americans that are not characteristic of other groups of Americans. Characteristic differences such as the uniquely Negro dialect captured so masterfully by the poetry of Paul Lawrence Dunbar, the frenzied religious expression described by W.E.B. Du Bois, and the emotional depth and force of the spirituals.

Particular elements of cultural inheritance can be accounted for in terms of race. The sense of race is a functional aspect of culture. This race sense helps to emphasize and accentuate the values which become the conscious and salient symbols and tradition of the culture. These emphasized values are operational in the culture making process, and explain the persistence or resistance of cultural traits. The dominant patterns in a given culture are set by these stressed values. Moreover, these dominant patterns become social norms around which social conformation converges and this eventually establishes the culture-type. The race sense determines the accentuated values, and the values, in turn, produce the persistence or resistance of certain culture-traits: that is, distinguishing qualities of the culture in terms of elements that are noticeably present or lacking. The persistence and resistance, or acceptance and rejection, of culture-traits—ways of acting, speaking, interrelating, worshipping, eating, expressing, and so on.—establishes a dominant pattern in a given culture. This dominant pattern consists of social norms to which members of the group conform. With sufficient conformity to those norms, a culture-type is eventually established.

Race, for Locke, functions as an established, customary and socially inherited pattern of thought, action or behavior. These patterns become distinguishing qualities or characteristics of a particular group over time: that is, they become cultural traits or culture-traits. These distinguishing patterns get established through a process of selectivity. The values of a group incline them toward accepting certain patterns of behavior, thought, and action, and rejecting others. Cultural groups manifest an affinity for some patterns over others, and those preferred, or those which prove more adaptive and functional are more firmly established and become indicative of the group. Moreover, this selective preference and resistance seems to increase, rather than decrease, with more frequent contacts across culture groups, and intensifies where there is greater complexity of cultural elements in a particular place. The weight of historical evidence shows most cultures to be significantly amalgamated. Culture, Locke claims, is the result of "the meeting and reciprocal influence of several culture strains, several ethnic contributions" in the majority of cases.

Two popular fallacies are nullified by this understanding of culture, the first, the notion that a single total culture can be ascribed to a single ethnicity. Second, the use of intrinsic rather than fusion values to interpret culture. In particular, the view that Locke endorses encourages the detachment of "political dominance from cultural productivity" and rejects the traditional view that the highest achievements of a mixed culture are the unique contribution of the ethnic group that enjoys political and economic dominance. He writes: "[e]specially does this newer view insist upon the dissociations of the claims of political dominance and cultural productivity, and combat the traditional view that all or even the best elements of a culture are the contribution of the ethnic group which in a mixed culture has political dominance and is in dynastic control."[46] This is an interesting and important idea to explore. In fact, it constitutes a third fallacy, namely, the belief that the (politically, economically, religiously, scientifically, militarily) dominant ethnicity within a composite culture is solely, or even principally, responsible for its highest cultural achievements. It is plausibly the case that not only past scientific opinion but also past and present lay opinions commit this fallacy.

Another avenue to explore is the effect of implicit reliance on this fallacious principle in the understanding of cultural contributions by non-dominant ethnic strains. Such contributions may not be fully appreciated due to the implicit assumption that having not been made by the dominant ethnic group their actual cultural significance may not be fully appreciated. Locke asserts that races can and ultimately must be compared in terms of "their relative and characteristic abilities and tendencies" with regard to their cultural origins, assimilation, survival, and institutional contributions.[47] This comparison must be rooted in objective parity of values and conditions. If an ethnic race or culture group in a pluralistic society wants to claim sole responsibility for its culture, then it must eliminate from that culture any and all elements not demonstrably the result of its creative influence, and claim only what remains as its own. Further, if one race wants to deny to another any credit for having appropriated or contributed to their shared culture, the former can only legitimately lay claim to those cultural elements which can be proved to be the product of their race after those attributable to other races have been removed, and this only assuming that such reductive attribution of racial grounds is possible. Locke claims that what is needed for the scientifically objective comparison of cultures are "intrinsic values for the interpretation of any culture, and strictly commensurate or equivalent values as a basis of comparisons between them."[48] Locke proposes a few methodological changes to the study of culture. Principal among them is "the application of the reconstructed notion of race as social in manifestation and derivation."[49]

C.　Imperialism and Political Conceptions of Race

Importantly, Locke distinguishes racial creeds and practices from racial conceptions, and further distinguishes racial conceptions between anthropological or social conceptions and political conceptions of race. Locke means by race creed, an action guiding set of concepts, beliefs, or aims concerning racial differentiation and practice that are held by a social group and usually transmitted across generations, or imposed by a dominant social group. Race creeds originate, motivate, and reinforce race practices.[50] Older forms of racialism, Locke contends, differ from contemporary conceptions insofar as the former were often instinctual practices not informed by a "doctrine of race," whereas a malevolent and specious justification of irrational practices and beliefs characterized the latter. Locke claims that race creeds are a modern invention.[51] Race practices are the individual and institutionalized behavioral norms that govern interactions between racialized individuals and between racialized groups. Political conceptions of race, argues Locke, are rooted in the political fortunes of groups. Locke maintains that political conceptions of race arise out of the imperial practices of nations. He writes:

> Now the conception of "inferior" races or "backward" races and of "advanced" races or "superior" races largely comes from the political fortunes and political capacity of peoples. So that [the] people that [have] not been successful in acquiring dominance, the people that have not been able to force their group [identity] upon another group, will be called the inferior people [.They] will be called the backward people, *even though it may be a historical fact that they have contributed more importantly to the civilization of which they are a part than the people that [have] been able to actually make the nominal political conquest and [hold] political power* (Emphasis mine).

> So that the ruling people will be the people who invariably dominate the group, not only dominate the group practically but control the actual class distinctions that may prevail in the group, making almost all of the subordinate status of race flow from their will and their traditions.[52]

Locke argues that the sense of a dominant race would not spring up from the innate instincts of people. Rather, the seemingly instinctual belief that one's race is dominant results from long periods of imperial and political race practices. This is seen in part by the fact that modern civilization is largely in the hands of people who have for centuries engaged in successful imperial practices. While he denies that the sense of a dominant race is innate, Locke does argue that such a sense stands in a causal relationship to practices of imperial dominance. As Locke sees it, imperial practices of dominance cause the sense of racial dominance; that is, long histories of successful subjugation of a people under modern imperial practices that effectively strip such people of their own cultural inheritance and forces on them the cultural forms and practices of the imperial peoples leads simultaneously to devaluing of the subjugated peoples and elevation of the politically successful group. In explaining the move from successful imperial domination to the formation of a dominant racial sense, or sense of racial superiority, Locke is compelled to rely largely on his experiences at the intellectual seat of European, specifically British Empire, namely, his time at Oxford and Cambridge.[53]

The resulting theory of Anglo-Saxon dominance is predicated on an important and unjustified, because unjustifiable, assumption that "Anglo-Saxon dominance is *due* [to] Anglo-Saxon superiority, and that Anglo-Saxon superiority is inherent and hereditary, and inherent and hereditary on the basis of race"[54] The dominant group holds up its accomplishment as the achievement of the entire social race, and takes pride in the extent to which it has dominated. This is the first instance of one of the undesirable ways that social races contribute to culture and civilization. One in which that contribution is seen as totalizing and the influence of a dominant ethnic race group is understood as ubiquitous throughout the culture, with the whole culture being attributed to the dominant group and subordinate groups understood only as more or less capable of adopting the culture of the dominant group. And where the culture or civilization is claimed to be tied to a particular social race, and membership in that race is set in practice as the criterion for full participation, you have the sort of racial division and exclusion that functions as an obstacle to cultural democracy and an appreciation of the cultural contributions of ethnoracial minorities.

Forced enslavement in a foreign country that results from the loss of domestic war is the most extraordinary form of rendition and one that almost of necessity lands those who suffer such a fate collectively, perpetually, and politically powerless in the societies where they are forced to reside. But one ought to be careful not to mistake a severely limited or nonexistent political capacity that results from an unfortunate and tragic circumstance for a social or cultural ineptitude due to any inherent inferiority. Locke is keenly aware that "the history of successful contacts not only breeds what we might call 'dominate' races, but the 'dominate' race becomes the 'political' race, the politically [powerful] people who can mold contacts their way."[55] The obvious trouble with this is that "the people who are lacking in this sense will not only be lacking in the capacities for this kind of racial or political dominance, but they will come under the more forceful control of what are political or dominate groups."[56]

Locke argues that the view that race causes culture, and provincial race creeds that identify culture with the dominant race are incompatible with pacifism and internationalism because they naturalize racial or cultural difference in a way that tends toward proprietorship and pride and the sorts of racial prejudice that rests upon the belief in a natural division between populations of human beings. The dilemma between provincial race creeds and practices on the one hand, and pacifism and internationalism on the other, is not merely logical, in fact, the two may not be strictly incompatible. Rather, it is the way that race is practiced that leads to the dilemma as a kind of practical incompatibility. Locke admits to having been a "race man" but thinks his activities as such compatible with the further development of internationalism and the approach toward universalism.[57] This may seem at first glance more problematic for the view that reads Locke as a kind of eliminativist. First of all, fostering a racial sense, stimulating racial consciousness, and reviving a lapsing racial tradition, all forms of race advocacy that Locke confesses to have engaged in, do not commit one to any particular ontological view of race. Second, one's advocacy of these things might be conditional and provisional. The instrumental usefulness of such activities need not be taken to reify certain existences. Third, the ontological view that Locke is committed to may impact what each of these three activities entails, that is, what each practically means.

Locke claims that "[i]t is not the facts of the existence of race which are wrong, but our attitudes towards those facts."[58] Such a claim appears to be at odds with other aspects of his philosophy of race. The claim, for example, that race is determinative of culture is a supposed fact, that Locke argues is false. So some supposed facts about race are wrong, and it is not merely our attitudes toward those facts which are mistaken. Locke worries whether one ought to identify, promote or advance the mode of living unique to a given culture, at the risk of perpetuating the sort of social division and conflict that usually attends race prejudice, chauvinistic race creeds, and provincial race practices? This concern is similar to one expressed by the Cuban Revolutionary thinker José Martí who was concerned that racism and racialism of any kind lead almost inevitably to social division of the sort that is inimical to the interests of an emerging American nation. Martí articulates a notion of "good racism," by which he means the invocation of racialism as a means of disproving pernicious race creeds and curtailing prejudicial race practices.[59] Take, for example, the claim that a past history of enslavement does not entail the inferior humanity of the enslaved population. Support for this claim is to be found in the fact that past enslavements of portions of the white race do not indicate white inferiority, not even in those cases where the white race was subjugated by the black race. This is an example of Martí's notion of good racism or racialism. Martí argues that good racism is pure justice.[60] Such implementations of good racialism are motivated by self-respect against claims of racial inferiority. Martí contends that the shedding of prejudice by whites is aided by good racism.[61] The right of members of the black race to prove and maintain their humanity, potential, capacity and rights is the limiting condition of just racism.

The concern for Locke, as well as Marti, is that in perpetuating racial idioms and race thinking one runs the risk of also furthering the negative consequences of racial creeds and practices. The issue then becomes whether there is a way to restrict and limit the use of racialism, such hat undesirable consequences can be avoided. In short, are there ameliorative invocations of racialism? Locke and Marti, answer in the affirmative, though Locke is arguably more permissive on this point han Marti. Locke's answer to this dilemma lies in what he sees as the "almost limitless natural reciprocity between cultures."[62] Civilizations, Locke notes, despite their many claims to distinctiveness, are vast amalgamations of cultures. That is, civilizations are constituted by the multiplicity of cultural contributions made by members of many populations, some even by cultural groups that constitute a social race. Racialism, in Locke's view, can be put to good or bad uses. An endorsement of racialism as it currently exists and the practices and attitudes that presently accompany it is ipso facto an endorsement of existing race creeds and the present racial order. However, if the consequences of racialism are not only negative, if racialism can be useful for beneficent social purposes, as Locke contends it can be, then, it seems that it ought to be endorsed. The troubling thing for Locke is the possibility of eliminating undesirable racial practices and preserving the desirable practices. If all political conceptions of race are scientifically false, then invocations of race meant to correct their theoretical inaccuracies are instances of good racialism. If reactions to political conceptions of race are instances of good racialism, then good racialism is appropriate in a larger range of circumstances than Martí seems to acknowledge.

Races, for Locke, are culture groups, characteristic culture-types that create specifically unique modes of living, forms of expression, and patterns of response. These can result in concrete patterns of activity and institutional forms, and myriad cultural and artistic products marked by particular idioms and themes. But in bearing the ethnoracial mark of a given population, these concrete cultural or racial goods are not the exclusive possession of the social race that created them. Both their very production and their functional utility across circumstances and contexts are caught up already with the multiplicity of intercultural relations and racial contacts that condition the social world. The ethnic race is not related to culture in terms of an ability or inability of the former to create the latter, nor as a limitation or possibility for the former to create and establish higher or lower, more or less sophisticated forms of the latter. Instead, race in the ethnic or social sense, imbues cultural goods with a particular consciousness, gives manifestation to a collective sense of identity, opens new possibilities for intercultural contacts, all without establishing for the social race that creates them, proprietary control over the goods themselves, and even less so over the source materials for these goods. Social races contribute to cultures a better understanding of their interrelations, new idioms of artistic and cultural expression, an expanded understanding of the culture elements that comprise the larger civilization that cultures have in common, and the conditions that set the possibility for a diversity of experiences and reciprocal exchanges of a genuinely cosmopolitan character. To be sure, cultures fail to realize the full benefits of ethnoracial contributions to culture as often as they take advantage of them. In fact, a great deal of Locke's work on race, culture and democracy centers around a concern for the aspects of our culture and cultural practices which function as obstacles to a saner pluralist, and cosmopolitan appreciation of ethnoracial contributions to American democracies.

D. Locke's Conception of Culture

> As serious-minded Americans we must all be thinking gravely and rigorously about the present state of the national culture and mindful of the special and yet unrealized demands of culture in a democratic setting. Perhaps it is truism but it is worth repeating that a few present liberal trends with the racial changes of popular attitude potentially involved are projecting helpful incentives toward a more democratic American culture. So far as the emancipation of the public mind from prejudice and group stereotypes, this may be properly regarded as, in large part, *a new Negro contribution to the broadening of the nation's culture.* But for us as Negroes, it is even more important to realize how necessary it is to share understandingly and participate creatively in these promising enlargements of the common mind and spirit. To be Democratic is as important as it is to be treated democratic; democracy is a two-way process and accomplish.[63]

Culture, for Locke, is a pragmatic and existential ideal (the same is true of his conception of democracy). He once believed that the notion of culture was more limited than the putative understanding.[64] As such it is not accessible to everyone, nor is it available to those who have access to it in the same degree. On Locke's earlier account, one does not inherit a culture simply by virtue of being born into it, one does not acquire culture, or become cultured so facilely; greater effort is required than the mere happenstance of accidental birth. In a 1923 essay, "The Ethics of Culture,"[65] Locke identifies education as the primary mechanism through which culture is transmitted. However, he notes that in this context the notion of education should not be construed to narrowly, "for in the best sense, and indeed in the most practical sense, it means not only the fitting of the man to earn his living, but to live and to live well."[66] Such an enabling of capacities for living fully and equally is definitive of culture on his view as "[i]t is just this latter and higher function of education, the art of living well...of living up to the best, that the word *culture* connotes and represents."[67] Locke goes so far as to offer "a touch-stone for this idea, a sure test of its presence"; namely, presence in education of "the purpose and motive of knowing better than the practical necessities of the situation demand, whenever the pursuit of knowledge is engaged in for its own sake and for the inner satisfaction it can give, culture and the motives of culture are present."[68]

Culture, on Locke's earlier view, is not the ubiquitous and inescapable social medium that it was for Dewey,[69] "[r]ather it is the capacity for understanding the best and most representative forms of human expression, and of expressing oneself, if not in similar creativeness, at least in appreciative reactions and in progressively responsive tastes and interests."[70] To be cultured on that account is in large part to acquire a set of dispositions and experiential mechanisms which enable one to engage with, appreciate, and emulate the instantiation of human excellence. But, Locke cautioned "[a]s faulty as is the tendency to externalize culture, there is still greater error in over intellectualizing it."[71] Being cultured, is for Locke a way of modifying experience, more specifically it is a way of modifying how and what one experiences. This is the internal dimension of culture, the dimension that relies on the individual's effort. The external dimension of culture has to do with features of the social environment and the cultured agent's experience of them.[72]

By the time that he delivers the lectures in Haiti, Locke's understanding of culture has matured and transformed in significant ways though it retains some of his earlier views on the subject. In the lectures, Locke turns his attention to the outmoded political conception of culture that has dominated the last century and a half. Before that, he claims the eighteenth century was marked by a more cosmopolitan cultural outlook. The paradoxical result being that as our world has become more interconnected by technology and communication, it has grown increasingly narrow in its conception of culture. He then takes up the task of articulating a better understanding of culture. Prevailing conceptions of nationalism in the nineteenth and early part of the last century obscured the facts of cultural history. Totalitarian conceptions of culture and notions of a master race were not the exclusive perspectives of Japanese, Nazi, and Italian racialists. The belief in the organic connection between race and culture—a belief at odds with Locke's philosophy of race—has been diffuse throughout the Americas and Europe, along with the belief that civilization was the exclusive product and procession of those nations and ethnic groups who happened to enjoy political and economic power and control. The older conception, that race causes culture, not only posits a false causal relationship between the two, on Locke's view, it confuses the proper direction of influence between the two notions. Locke's view claims the inverse, that race is a product of culture. Arguably, the view is even stronger than that, i.e. that culture determines, perhaps even causes, race. The facts, Locke states, run contrary to such beliefs, but only a few more scientifically minded observers were able to grasp a broader notion of cultural kinship.[73]

One is prompted to stop, says Locke, to consider why full democracy as a way of life is still so far from being generally recognized.[74] American conceptions of nationality still preserve the European tradition of associating nationality with culture. This practice is to be found throughout the Americas. Locke claims that America's cultures must build upon existing American realities, not outmoded European stereotypes. It is incumbent upon American nations, Locke thinks, to reject competitive nationalism and cultivate and promote a pluralistic civilization that can merge political nationalism and cultural pluralism in a way that can be at home in the increasingly international world. A major aspect of Locke's entire philosophical outlook is concerned with identifying the fundamental impediments to forming appropriate value attitudes and orientations toward the goods of humanity; in particular, full and free expression of one's personhood, on grounds of reciprocity and mutual respect, as members of equal standing in cosmopolitan democratic cultures, and cultivating the effective means of ameliorating the obstacles to such a social arrangement and practice. As pertains to these lectures, the impediments in question are those that forestall an accurate understanding of race, culture, and democracy and all three in their interconnections throughout the Americas. For purposes of the subject of the lectures, those impediments are parochialism, racial chauvinism, and provincialism.[75]

Locke argues that provincialism is deeply rooted in various American cultures. Political efforts to achieve a larger democratic ideal, or cultural democracy, need to be reinforced by a moral or spiritual conviction in equality and fraternity between various social groups. Such a conviction requires the transformation of our provincialisms.[76] We retain our provincialisms because they assert our uniqueness and superiority to others.[77]

If the democratic ideal of cultural democracy is to be obtained, then we must have a moral and spiritual conviction in group parity. We will not have a moral and spiritual conviction in group parity unless we jettison or transform our provincialisms. So, if the democratic ideal of cultural democracy is to be obtained, then we must jettison or transform our provincialisms. Locke comments on an important aspect of this transformation when he writes:

The most obvious, as well as the most important, is that there is no room for any consciously maintained racialism in matters cultural. The generation to which I belong had to do more than its normal share of defensive, promotive propaganda for the Negro but it is my greatest pride that I have never written or edited a book on a chauvinistically racialist basis. Seldom has farsighted Negro scholarship or artistry proceeded on such a basis and today racialism cannot and should not be tolerated. We can afford to be culturally patriotic but never culturally jingoistic.[78]

Another major obstacle to transforming our provincialisms is that we believe they assert our uniqueness and superiority to others.[79] If we were to disabuse ourselves of the belief that they did, we would be much less inclined to retain them. Locke believes this becomes possible when such beliefs are shown to be false. Moreover, if there were a viable substitute for narrow-mindedness in this regard, we might in becoming less biased be more willing to adopt that alternative. Locke proposes two alternatives: first, is an emphasis on commonality (common features across cultures), what he elsewhere calls basic values, or cultural constants. Second, is an accurate appreciation of difference: that is, understanding the distinction between a basic or functional difference, and a mere difference of form. What grounds Locke's application of his axiology to a relative assessment of cultures is the principle that cultures ought only to be compared in terms of commensurate or in some way—either basically or functionally—equivalent values.[80] Conversely, it follows that if any two values across cultures fail to be commensurate or equivalent, they ought not to be used as the basis for comparison. In case they are, the relative judgments, to some extent, lose their claims to scientific objectivity. If a culture wishes to deny the influence of an ethnic group that has contributed to their culture, then they must, for objective parity's sake, deny the influence of all other ethnic groups on the culture and claim as distinctively theirs, only what little residue remains.

In a later essay, "The Frontiers of Culture," Locke urges that we "take for granted, if it hasn't been conclusively proven, that culture has no color, that although Negro life and experience should have and are having increased and increasingly effective expression, there is no monopoly, no special proprietary rights, no peculiar credit and no particular needs or benefits about culture."[81] He further notes the incongruity of the dominant provincial conception of nationality with the realities of American states, which are typically made of racially diverse populations with multi-national cultural origins.[82] The newer nations of the Americas do not need to "make the mistake of projecting Old World patterns and traditions upon an essentially new type of culture."[83] Locke claims that for American societies to do so is contrary to "their own basic structure," and forestalls "the development of their potentialities as pioneers of that cosmopolitan culture typical of complete democracy and of an increasingly international world."[84] Evidence of the obfuscating effect of the myth of a single racial origin of culture or civilization can be seen in the disconnect between that view and the actual facts of cultural development in the United States and Afrodescendant people's influence on that development, or the influence of indigenous peoples in Canada on Canadian national culture.[85]

Locke concludes from such examples and from a survey of the actual facts of America's cultures that monolithic American cultures are few and far between, if they exist at all, and that the longstanding and predominant pattern in the Americas is one of the composite cultures with a multiplicity of racial, ethnic, religious, and national geneses. He further concludes that "[o]n that basis, then, all we should be concerned about is freer participation and fuller collaboration in the varied activities of the cultural life and with regard both to the consumer and the producer roles of cultural creation. Democracy in culture means equally wide-scale appreciation and production of the things of the spirit."[86]

E. Afrodescendant Peoples' Cultural Contributions to Art and Literature

In view of the dramatic yet integral character of the Negro's life with that of the dominant majority, and especially in view of the complementary character of the dominant Negro traits with those of Anglo-Saxon Nordic, it would seem to be a situation of profitable exchange and real cultural reciprocity. For the Negro's predisposition toward the artistic, promising to culminate in a control and mastery of the spiritual and mystic as contrasted with the mechanical and practical aspects of life, makes him a spiritually needed and culturally desirable factor in American life. However, for the general working out of such a delicate interaction of group psychologies we cannot predict, but can only await the outcome of what is historically and sociologically a unique situation. All that we can be sure of in advance is the positive and favorable internal effect of such recent cultural development upon the course of Negro group life itself.[87]

There are some important preliminaries to a thorough consideration of the ethnoracial contribution of Afrodescendant peoples to American cultures. Aside from a clear understanding of the relationship between ethnic race and culture, which has been considered above, there is the question of the formers ability to exert an influence on the latter; along with the question of what qualifies as the unique product of a given ethnoracial group, and the appropriate desiderata for making such a determination. In a 1928 literary review essay entitled "The Negro's Contribution to American Art and Literature," Locke offers a historical record and theoretical analysis of African American cultural products in the USA. Locke asserts that the cultural background of African descendant people in the USA is characterized by two basic elements: one, a historically vague and obscured primitive African heritage, and two, the unique character of their experiences in the USA and the specific social conditions under which that experience historically unfolded. Moreover, the phenotypic distinctiveness of African Americans, a fact that makes the conditions of their lives nearly "inescapable for all sections of the Negro population, and function, therefore, to intensify emotionally and intellectually group feelings, group reactions, and group traditions."[88] Locke writes:

> Such *an accumulating body of collective experience inevitably matures into a group culture which just as inevitably finds some channels of unique expression, and this has been and will be the basis of the Negro's characteristic expression of himself in American life.* In fact, as it matures to conscious control and intelligent use, what has been the Negro's social handicap and class liability will very likely become his positive group capital and cultural asset. Certainly whatever the Negro has produced thus far of distinctive worth and originality has been derived in the main from this source, with the equipment from the general stock of American culture acting at times merely as the precipitating agent; at others, as the working tools of this creative expression (Emphasis mine).[89]

An "accumulating body of collective experience" is the incipient stage of group cultural formation, which as it coalesces into unique and specifiable forms of expression, becomes distinguishable as an ethnic race. This is the only potentially positive form of racial differentiation his view can countenance. For Locke, race is uniquely expressive of culture. His philosophy of race rules out the possibility that putative racial populations cause or otherwise determine specific cultural formations. Culture on his view is produces ethnic race, not vice versa.

The cultural history of the African Americans in the United States, Locke claims, is unique and dramatic. African Americans were severed from their native cultures and forced into complex and foreign cultures and civilization. Those alien cultures and civilizations forced upon African descendant peoples in the USA, European languages, Christianity, systems of forced labor, and Latin and Anglo-Saxon customs and norms. More so is this seen with an Inter-American approach to African descendant peoples in the Americas. Anglo, Spanish, French, and Portuguese cultures are all adopted and appropriated to various degrees by African descendant people in the Americas. This is particularly telling in regard to perhaps the most noteworthy fact to Locke about African cultural history in the Americas; namely, their "complete mental and spiritual flexibility."[90] It was this, according to Locke, that enabled the rapid assimilation of the newly encountered cultures in the Americas by African peoples. Locke observes that such assimilation often took place within the first generation and that is "almost without parallel in history."[91] The assimilative capacity of African Americans notwithstanding, Locke notes that an "African and racial temperament" was present in the most insipient attempts at self-expression, and this imbued African American life and action with peculiar and characteristic qualities. He writes:

> I can give a concrete illustration by indicating what we are starting to know of African music, now that we can trace its various branches and variants, placing them one next to the other ... Similarities in rhythm, in cadence, tone intervals between Afro-Brazilian popular songs, Afro-Cuban, Afro-Antillean, and Afro-American, have provided researchers with their initial evidence, the means to do better analysis of the music of West African tribes, and these have in turn provided a basis which, for the first time, convincingly explains some common characters of American variants .... We are able to see that, after being mixed here with French musical themes, there with Spanish themes, and in other circumstances, with Anglo-Saxon themes, and even with mixtures of these complex themes, there remain many different elements that are distinctly African and ancestral. These common characteristics show, in addition, two particularly important facts: on the one hand, they reveal the wide range of the African musical influence, and on the other hand show its versatile but expansive potential. The African musical influence has left its mark on much of the New World, from the Caribbean to the Eastern states of the United States in terms of the North, and Brazil and Venezuela to Peru, in terms of the South.[92]

The first and most basic contribution by Afrodescendant people to American culture came by way of the generally unacknowledged influence of black idioms on Southern white culture.[93] The subject matter of Afrodescendant expressions was genuinely American, yet the specific patterns and designs by way of language, social temperament, creativity, and spirituality were ethnoracially African American. The transmission and influence may have come through the medium of condescending imitation, but the impact and effect were no less real or significant. In fact, this observation leads Locke to a fundamental principle grounding his understanding of ethnoracial contributions to culture. "The principle of *cultural reciprocity*," which Locke states, involves "a general recognition of the reciprocal character of all contacts between cultures and of the fact that all modern cultures are highly composite ones," an understanding that Locke thinks more accurately reflects the reality of American cultural formations and "would invalidate the lump estimating of cultures in terms of generalized, *en bloc* assumptions of superiority and inferiority, substituting scientific, point-by-point comparisons with their correspondingly limited, specific, and objectively verifiable superiorities of inferiorities."[94]

Against the tendency to think that cultural influences are always an effect of a dominant culture on a subordinate one, Locke notes "[i]t is a fallacy that the overlord influences the peasant and remains uninfluenced by him; and in this particular case, with the incorporation of the Negro into the heart of the domestic life of the South, the counter-influence became particularly strong."[95] This is an important principle that Locke unearths in his consideration of African American cultural contributions in the United States. Cultural and ethnoracial influence is often a two-way process. The socially, politically, and economically disadvantaged groups in a society are not always the passive receivers of the dominant group culture. Groups that hold social, political, or economic advantage can also be influenced by the groups relative to whom they hold a dominant position. More so is this understood when one grasps Locke's position that supposed racial superiority is, in fact, the result of imperial success on the part of an ethnic race, and not the manifestation of any innate superiority. As political, economic, and imperial success are not due to inherent racial capacities, and claims to the contrary reflected only the privileges that attach to certain kinds of success in these areas coupled with provincial racial creeds that allow dominant groups to claim proprietary possession of a given culture; there is reason to think that the influences of subcultural groups and contributions to a given culture extend beyond the group that is politically dominant. What is more, integration of cultural elements does not have to be an intentional or positive phenomenon. Cultural elements can be integrated through mocking condescension, forced acquiescence, or stubborn persistence. So, the mere fact that a people and their ways are held in generally low regard is not an absolute impediment to an incorporation of their characteristic modes of action by the groups that so regard them.

Afrodescendant folk ways have impacted the sense of humor, emotional attitude, superstitious beliefs, insouciance, congeniality, sentiment and illogicality first of the South, and over time the entire nation. More than that, African American cultural modes, those Locke terms Negro, have influenced, among other things, United States law, political and economic organization, educational institutions and practices, various forms of political protest and activism, as well as the practice of various religions and idioms of public oratory. Locke credits the popularity and appeal of jazz, in his own time with helping to spread, at least superficially, the cultural influence of African Americans. Initially, the main influence was on folk cultural ways, coming over time to constitute the subject matter of more refined and formally cultivated artistic forms. But Locke notes that is as important to affect a nation's sense of humor, style of dance, the pace of its life, and its folklore and folks songs, as it is to shape its formal poetry, fiction or art. African American artistic expression began with folk forms of expression. Control over the formal modes of artistic expression would come later. It was inevitable, claims Locke, that the specific experiences of Afrodescendant populations in the United States would be expressed artistically. Folk dance, lore and song, especially the spirituals, provided the raw materials for a genuinely African American art in the United States. Young artists in the United States in the first quarter of the twentieth century began to recognize the extent quality and originality of this rich cultural resource. Much of that cultural material was the product of slavery, which gave to African American art a range of human emotion, and depth of spiritual and emotional feeling scarcely to be found anywhere else in North American culture. "Paradoxically enough," Locke observes, "it may be that in slavery the Negro made American civilization permanently his spiritual debtor."[96]

Locke divides the cultural history of African descendant peoples in the USA into two broad time periods: The first began with the introduction of African peoples to the Americas and was characterized primarily by folk expression. The second stretches back intermittently to 1787, having become semi-literary from 1835 to 1860 with the anti-slavery movement, and becoming fully literary since 1890. The span between these two periods was filled by a transitional period where emulation of methods and criteria in the USA typify black expression. During this time, Locke claims, there was a move toward an attempt at conformity with prevailing conventions. Locke writes off that attempt as normal and inevitable under the circumstances. The attempt at cultural conformity was reversed in the period since 1890, first by the dialect poetry and folklore of Paul Laurence Dunbar, and then by the "New Negro movement."

Locke credits the "New Negro movement" with having produced a considerable volume of, and the highest quality, contributions to American literature and art. This movement caused a reorientation of racial sentiment and group attitude, and established "a national literature in the vernacular upon the educated classes of other peoples, who also at one or another stage of their cultural development were not integrated with their own particular tradition and folk-background."[97] Locke claims that the general history of white Anglo-American acceptance of the cultural traits and elements of African Americans followed the same general pattern. At first, there was a long period of reciprocal interchange that likely began out of sentimental curiosity, and that was followed by a general disdain and condescension through the growth of slavery. Second, there came a more formal revulsion, in part an attempt to culturally isolate African descendant peoples, and in part a symptom of the raging slavery versus abolition debate. This continued through reconstruction. The third stage began around 1895 with a renascent and objective interest in African American cultural elements and themes in the USA as the more general trend in American realism continued to grow. Many of the leading literary figures in the USA paid considerable attention to the materials and folk-themes of African American life. This use of cultural materials by white literary figures was at times exploitive, but has also encouraged the use of those cultural materials more widely, and even at times provided a backhanded vindication of African American source material. There also developed new sites of cultural contact and mutual influence and cooperation between both races.

Locke claims that the more the Negro is understood culturally rather than sociologically, the more it is recognized by black and white alike that African American cultural products in the USA are culturally fine, and of tremendous value to the national art. The spirituals and Uncle Remus tales, Locke asserts, are sufficient proof. A good deal of Afrodescendant cultural material has been lost to the ages, he laments, but efforts have

been undertaken to reclaim some of that lost past. With their own sentimental additions which the literary scholarship of his day had yet to separate from the original African American folktales, Locke names Cable,
Thomas Nelson Page, and Joel Chandler Harris as (white) American writers who helped to popularize that folklore.

It was African descendant people in the United States themselves who
preserved their folk music, notably the spirituals. The Fisk Jubilee Singers
undertook great effort to reclaim much of the African American musical
past, resurrecting it in one form or another, even if only in spirit. This
effort has resulted, since 1900, in the work of notable musicians such as
Harry T. Burleigh, S. Coleridge-Taylor, Rosamond Johnson, Carl Ditton,
Nathaniel Dett, Lawrence Brown, Edward Boatner, William Grant Still,
and C. S. Ballanta.

Secular African American music began with a period of sentimental treatment as evidenced by the melodies of Stephen Foster, and from around
the 1850s until the 1890s was marked by minstrel balladry, until finally
jazz began to exert a constant and at times dominant influence on popular music and dance in the United States. The popular forms of African
American music in the United States were according to Locke, somewhat
debased forms of their folk originals, and this was so whether in the hands
of white or black professional musicians. The fact that the authentic forms
were able to withstand this appropriation proves, by Locke's lights, just
how superb they were in the first instance. Scholarship in Locke's day
had come to their rescue by way of uncovering, cataloging, and transcrib-
ing the folk music of Afrodescendant peoples in the United States, and
this scholarship by such notable musicians and scholars as Odum, Weldon
Johnson, and Ballanta make it possible to "judge the genuine worth and
tone of the Negro folk-product."[98] Locke says further, "[f]inely representative as they are in their historical time and setting, they are now regarded
as even more precious in their potential worth as material for fresh artistic
development."[99]

In commenting on the literary contribution of Frederick Douglas,
Locke writes:

> Slavery, which a brilliant ex-slave called "the graveyard of the mind," did
> not prove to be a tomb of the spirit; the Negro soul broke through to
> two ideals,—heaven and freedom,—and expressed these hopes imperish-
> ably. Although this was an expression of his own particular situation and his
> specific reactions, it was so profoundly intense as to become universalized;

spiritually there are no finer expressions of belief in freedom and immortality, or of the emotional side of Christianity native to the American soil than
these Negro folk utterances.[100]

If slavery transformed and shaped the emotional life of Afrodescendant
people in the United States, Locke claims, it was the effort to abolish it
that cultivated the black intellect and occasioned eloquent expression of
African American thought and character. The literary efforts of African
Americans in the United States began during the period of chattel slavery, hampered of course by heavy constraint of intellectual opportunities.
Not excepting the important role that has been discussed of the oral folk
tradition of African descendant peoples, Locke tends to mark the beginning of the African American literary tradition in the United States by
the exceptional literary efforts of the likes of Phyllis Wheatley and Jupiter
Hammond, and the slave Narratives of people like Olaudah Equiano
(Gustavus Vassa).

This incipient African American literature was followed by protest literature characteristic of abolitionist writing such as David Walker's *Appeal to
the Colored Citizens of the World*,[101] Maria W. Stewart's speeches and edi-
torials, the autobiographies of Frederick Douglas, and the work of Henry
Highland Garnett. Locke writes that "[f]rom this point on the growing
anti-slavery movement developed necessarily the second-rate literature
of controversy."[102] In these notable instances, Locke acknowledges that
these writers "all developed stages beyond literacy to forceful and pol-
ished oratory, and occasionally into matured scholarship."[103] Locke takes
a sober view of anti-slavery literature, remaining ever careful not to overes-
timate its merits. The abolitionist writing of African and Anglo-American
authors alike is "admittedly second-rate," according to Locke, though the
literature's historical representativeness of a particular cultural context is
undeniable. The Negro literature of the period Locke claims was mostly
imitative, seeking to conform to mainstream idioms, though here and
there characteristic features were on display. Slave narratives, he claims,
were the most original products by Negro authors during this period.
There were also anti-slavery poets, the likes of George Horton and Francis
Ellen Watkins Harper.

To be sure, Locke did not think the literature was second rate in itself,
but rather seems to have thought that its reactionary or apologetic quality diminished its quality as purely expressive. He makes clear that he
thought highly of these literary efforts when he writes, "[y]et in this and

the allied field of oratory, the Negro contribution was exceptional and at times up to the level of contemporary white talent, Garrison, Jay, Gerritt Smith, Sumner Phillips, as a critical comparison of the orations and essays of Martin Delany, Samuel McCune Smith, Thomas Remond, Ringgold Ward, Henry Highland Garnett, Edward Wilmot Blyden, the West Indian scholar and abolitionist, and the greatest popular figure of the group, Frederick Douglass will show."[104]

The pervasiveness of slavery as a growing political and economic problem hampered the range of expressiveness that African American writers in the United States could engage in and display. So long as slavery existed as a system, Afrodescendant people were not fully human. But more to the point, the abolition of the institution was required in order for African American writers to be able to turn their attention to other human concerns.

In comparison to folk expressions and the powerfully emotive spirituals Locke views African American abolitionist literature as "painfully self-conscious effusions of sentimental appeal and moral protest" that are relatively tame and primarily of historical interest.[105] The value he sees in this early phase of African American literature is that it brought the African American intellect into mastery of the English language, articulate expression, and into contact with mainstream practical and cultural contact. African American literary talent during this period was not wholly confined to social protest literature. There were also, during this period, significant contributions to *belles lettres* from the likes of Martin Delany, Henry Highland Garnett, William Wells Brown, and Frank Webb. Energy from this protest literature was drained by the coming of the Civil War and later Reconstruction, and the creative energies of Afrodescendant intellectuals in the United States were primarily devoted to more practical concerns during this era. After 1875, white writers in the United States began to produce sentimental glorifications of the "Old South" in the absence of any counter-response by white Northern writers.[106] Meanwhile, African American writers took to revising slave autobiographies and "propounding panaceas for the solution of the race question."[107]

During this time, Locke claims, a considerable amount of historical data was accumulated on Afrodescendant people in the United States. But simultaneously, the literature of white Southerners was equally sentimental and worked to produce many of the most pernicious stereotypes that continue to characterize African Americans in the United States. This continued through the work of figures such as Cable, Harris, and Nelson

Page further reifying the violently propagandistic and caricaturist treatment of Afrodescendant people in North American literature culminating in the work of Thomas Dixon.[108]

Locke attributes the recovery of African American literary effort after the 1880s, primarily to the literary efforts of Charles Waddell Chestnutt and Paul Lawrence Dunbar, whose work countered the stereotypes of the preceding period. The dialect poetry for which Dunbar was so famous, and did a great deal to popularize, was also a source of controversy. On Locke's assessment, "[t]here is no question about the representativeness of Dunbar's happy-go-lucky, self-pitying peasant; it is only a matter of realizing two things,—that he stands for the race at a certain stage of its history and a certain class at that stage."[109] Locke regards Dunbar as an end rather than a beginning of a literary era, occupying a transitional period between the protest literature of the abolitionist movement and turn of the century intellectualism. As Dunbar continued to grow in popularity so did the dialect school of poetry.

In the period from 1895 to 1905, the controversy over the opposing race programs of Washington and Du Bois created a cleavage between the masses of African Americans and the more affluent and educated class. The dialect school of poetry and other more realistic forms of expression were assigned to the Washington side. The literary efforts of Du Bois became the paradigmatic representation of the opposing side. Locke takes note of the propagandistic and protest elements of this literature, but also attributes to it a significant role in advancing the cause of cultural equality, and helping to resurrect the motivation for pure self-expression and other cultural pursuits. On the non-propagandist side, he attributes to Dunbar the inclusion in American literature of "the important genre figure of the Negro peasant and troubadour-minstrel."[110] Roundabout 1912–1915 a transformation began to unfold. The intellectualist school headed by Du Bois was accompanied by the emergence of a more self-expressive school of newer poetry. Du Bois was of course importantly influential in the literature of this time, but Locke attributes an equal and perhaps greater indirect influence to the career and work of William Stanley Braithwaite. Braithwaite's own verses as well as his scholarly anthologies served to encourage the production of poetry and art for its own sake, and with the rise of poetry, in that vein, there was a corresponding decline in dialect poetry. Then in the period from 1917 to 1922 figures such as James Weldon Johnson, Fenton Johnson, Charles Bertran, Roscoe Jameson, Georgia Douglas Johnson, and Claude McKay revived African American artistic production of the highest rate. The art of this period was characterized by its use of the African American experience in the USA as the starting point of artistic expression. African American source material was universalized: that is, shown through the use of traditional poetic forms and symbols to be a paragon of humanity. Earlier themes of social protest continued in this literature in a refined and dignified way. Exaltation of the "racial background" was a dominant aspect of this literature, along with that of "racial types of beauty."[111]

The same turn away from propagandistic motives toward truer artistic expression that took place in literature, took place in music. The artistic potential of the Spirituals and other folk musical forms was revived by the freer expression of artistry. This phase of African American music, and art more generally, Locke claims, was not primarily motivated by the realism prevalent in the larger American culture and the growing fascination with Afrodescendant folk materials; instead, it was driven by "a new desire for representative group expression" that paralleled the enlivening of African American life in the United States that came as a result of greater education and economic advancement.[112]

It was this trend toward "racial self-expression and cultural autonomy" that Locke labeled the New Negro movement in 1925 with the publication of a special issue of *Survey Graphic*.[113] Locke writes:

> Since then the accumulated spiritual momentum of one knows not how many generations has suddenly precipitated in a phenomenal burst of creative expression in all the arts, poetry and music leading as might be expected, but with very considerable activity in the fields of fiction, race drama, Negro history, painting, sculpture and the decorative arts. It is a sound generalization to say that three-fourths of the total output is avowedly racial in inspiration and social objective, that a good part of it aims at the capitalization of the folk materials and the spiritual products of the group history; and equally safe to assert that more worth-while artistic output and recognition have been achieved in less than a decade than in all the range of time since 1619.[114]

The Harlem Renaissance came at the same time as increased interest in African American experience in the United States by white artists. Locke was initially cautious that the full cultural and social effect of the New Negro movement would not be fully manifest "for half a generation yet."[115] Though cautious he thought the movement already showed the potential to achieve the cultural significance of folk revivals in the Irish Renaissance of the Celtic tradition, or the Czechoslovakian use of Bohemian history. In the case of the Harlem Renaissance it held out hope of purely artistic expression and endeavors, and the encouragement of cultural equality. One notable result of the Harlem Renaissance was the wider inclusion of African Americans as contributors to the national culture and a partner in the expression of the national character.

The poetry, fiction, sculpture, and painting of younger New Negro artist manifests not only a capacity for sophisticated emotional and technical control but also a critical social insight and analysis. African American artists were able to match technical mastery with an intimate acquaintance with the reality and feeling of the African American experience in the USA giving them priority over the use of the black experience as artistic material, though, to the benefit of North American art generally, not exclusive control.[116] Purely artistic expression of African American life is an important milestone in the cultural assimilation of Afrodescendant people in the United States. For one, artistic expression of the sort Locke has in mind is able to transform the substance, tone, emotion, spirituality of people's folk culture into products that are universally illustrative of aspects of the human condition. Unlike prior literature, which created stereotypes of African American culture and personality, the more genuine art showed African descendant people in a truer light.

In 1928, Locke began to wonder whether as African Americans continued to gain recognition as an integral part of the North American culture, the most important and influential contributions to the culture of the United States would come in the form of its artistic creations or the cultural and social off shoots of those creations. Locke writes: "[a]part from the great actual and potential effects of this self-expression upon group morale and inner stimulation, there is that equally important outer effect which may actually bring about a new cultural appraisal and acceptance of the Negro in American life."[117] On the question of African American cultural contributions in the United States Locke claims that "America, in fact, has never psychologically spurned the Negro or been cold to the spiritual elements of his temperament; it is simply a question now of what reactions their expression on a new and advanced level will generate in a situation where both products and producer must together be accepted or rejected, deprecated or recognized."[118]

F. Racial Cultural Contributions: Understanding the Place of Afrodescendant Peoples in the Americas' Cultures

Having provided a comprehensive historical and theoretical account of African American artistic contributions to the culture of the United States, and establishing thereby the type and extent of Afrodescendant people's roles in the evolution of that culture, deeper considerations concerning how that history relates to Locke's conceptions of ethnic race and culture remain. The question, then, is when affixed adjectivally to the term "art" what does the word "Negro" add to one's understanding of a particular cultural product or contribution? Locke's later concern is not with whether or not there are cultural contributions and products that have been made by African descendant peoples to the larger culture in the United States; rather, it is what, if anything makes them distinctively racial? Thus, what is being sought after is not historical evidence of artistic or intellectual products created by Afrodescendant people—that much is given at this point—nor sociological or ethnological proof of their influence on American civilization—that too, is easily observed. Instead, what an answer to Locke's query demands is an account of the racial uniqueness and distinctiveness of these products and contributions or their creators. Are such artifacts and influences peculiar to a particular population, or are they authentically and fully a part of the culture of the United States? Locke writes:

> After twenty years or so of continuous discussion, this subject of the cultural contribution of the Negro as a racial group has become quite trite and well-nigh threadbare. Having undergone much critical wear and tear, and having passed in the process from intriguing novelty to tawdry commonplace and from careful critical delineation to careless propaganda, the whole subject now obviously needs, even to the layman's eye, thoroughgoing renovation. Before we proceed to any further documentation, then, of the Negro's cultural contributions, let us address ourselves to this more difficult task of its critical evaluation.[119]

Where that leaves one then, is face-to-face with Locke's famous query: "Who, and What, is Negro?"[120]

In a 1939 article, "The Negro's Contribution to American Culture," Locke reasons that even if one grants that the very concept of African American art or cultural contributions are consequences of racial discrimination and minority status, this does not entail that "an uncritical acceptance of the situation is necessary or advisable."[121] The issue on Locke's estimation is characterized by a paradox: namely, what is the desiderata for a work of art or cultural contribution to count as African American, the ethnoracial identity of its author, its thematic subject matter, or its mode of expression?

Locke, of course, answers his own query when he remarks that "[w]hat is racial for the American Negro resides merely in the overtones to certain fundamental elements of culture common to white and black and his by adoption and acculturation."[122] So that what distinguishes ethnic races on his view, as has been shown above, are qualitative and characteristic variations on styles of living, divergent degrees and methods of expressiveness, variegated sensibilities, contrasting degrees of religiosity and spiritual comportment, and of course the more quotidian domains of living involved in cooking, speaking, child-rearing, and the various elements of folk culture. "What is distinctively Negro in culture," Locke continues, "usually passes over by rapid osmosis to the general culture, and often as in the case of Negro folklore and folk music and jazz becomes nationally current and representative."[123] Social races, as Locke understands them, are transitory; which is not to deny them any reality; rather it is to emphasize that ethnic races are transactional phenomena; and as such their reality is partially constituted through the interactions and interrelations between populations, as much as they are internally fortified. And this phenomenon is not unique to Afrodescendant people in the United States, or throughout the Americas for that matter as "[i]ncidentally, it is by the same logic and process that the English language, Anglo-Saxon institutions and mores, including English literary and art forms and traditions have become by differential acculturation what we style "American.""[124]

> In culture, it is the slightly but characteristically divergent that counts, and in most cases racial and nationalist distinctions are only shades of degrees apart. The Negro cultural product we find to be in every instance itself a composite, partaking often of the nationally typical and characteristic as well, and thus something which if styled Negro for short, is more accurately to be described as "Afro-American." In spite, then, of the ready tendency of many to draw contrary conclusions, there is little if any evidence and justification for biracialism in the cultural field, if closely scrutinized and carefully interpreted. The subtle interpenetration of the "national" and "racial" traits is interesting evidence of cultural cross-fertilization and the wide general vogue and often national representativeness of the 'racial contribution' is similar of the effective charm and potency of certain cultural hybrids.[125]

Locke argues that both positions at either extreme suffer from a similar fallacy, namely, the tendency of cultural racialism to lapse into cultural chauvinism, with equally disastrous effects on both horns of the dilemma. From the minority position, the fallacy of cultural racialism threatens to isolate African Americans from the United States' culture. Locke writes,

> Although there is in the very nature of the social situation an unavoidable tendency for the use of literature and art as instruments of minority group expression and counter-assertion, there is a dangerous fallacy of the minority position involved in cultural racialism. Cultural chauvinism is not unique in a racial situation, however; a national literature and art too arbitrarily interpreted has the same unpardonable flaws. However, where as in the case of the Negro there are no group differentials of language or basic culture patterns between the majority and the minority, cultural chauvinism is all the more ridiculous and contrary to fact. Consistently applied it would shut the minority up in a spiritual ghetto and deny vital and unrestricted creative participation in the general culture.[126]

So that authorship for example, if chosen as the criterion of African American artistic and cultural endowments, when coupled with racialism threatens to perpetuate ethnoracial identity as a barrier to inclusion in the wider culture in the United States, and relegate African American cultural goods to a marginalized province outside the mainstream culture. If specific subject matter or modes of expression are used as the criterion of African American art, then a consciously maintained racialism might tend toward a sense of ethnoracial proprietorship in terms of cultural products; a sense that the subject matter in question is the exclusive purview of Afrodescendant peoples. "On the other hand," Locke continues, "there is the majority fallacy of regarding a group like the Negro after the analogy of a 'nation within a nation,' implying a situation of different culture levels or traditions,"[127] that segregate Afrodescendant peoples and leave them outside the cultural fray. But, Locke warns "[s]ooner or later the critic must face the basic issues involved in his use of risky and perhaps untenable terms like 'Negro art' and 'Negro literature' and answer the much-evaded question unequivocally,—who and what is Negro?"[128] Furthermore, it is a meaningful query to ask whether the racial concept has any place in art at all. Locke suspects that it might be better to understand art as a cultural or social mode of production that cuts across racial and ethnic divisions.

Locke's answer to the query "Who is Negro?" begins by exposing a common and misguided assumption; he claims, "[t]he fallacy of the "new" as of the "older" thinking is that there is a type Negro who, either qualitatively or quantitatively, is the type symbol of the entire group."[129] This is the unfortunate consequence of the past need to proffer counter-stereotypes to combat demeaning stereotypes of African Americans. Some element of truth may well be contained in counter-stereotypes, but they necessarily fail to convey the whole truth about as diverse a population as Afrodescendant people in the United States, let alone the Americas, or the World. No distinctive singular African American type exists. So much more thoroughly is this understood through an Inter-American consideration of Afrodescendant peoples across the Americas than even a consideration of the diversity of African American life in any single nation would reveal. Locke's conception of ethnic race is devoid of any reliance on misguided biological suppositions, and provides a framework for understanding the ethnoracial variation within a putative racial category; people of African descendant for example. African Americans are a dynamic and multifaceted population admitting of myriad cultural and social forms characterized by variegated linguistic, religious and artistic elements. As African Americans of his day were thought to be classless, undifferentiated, and ethnically homogeneous it is a significant feature of Locke's Inter-American ethnoracial outlook that he undermines in many ways the arbitrary criteria of ethnoracial membership prevalent in the United States, and even in other parts of the Americas. In fact, Locke himself thought it possible (and actual) for human beings biologically similar in the way that American race thinking presupposes to be members of different races. A full and accurate artistic portrayal of who is Negro would, Locke argued, have to picture the many diverse Negro strands in their own right, weaving together from these diverse threads a multifaceted presentation of Negro experiences.

"Turning to the other basic question,—what is Negro," Locke begins by narrowing the question to "what makes a work of art Negro, if indeed any such nomenclature is proper,—its authorship, its theme or its idiom?"[130] In other words, what gives a particular work of art its distinctive, if any, ethnoracial character: the ethnic racial identity of its author, its treatment of themes characteristic of a particular ethnoracial experience in a particular place, or its use of styles and modes of expression peculiar to a given people? Of these three candidates for the foundation of African American art, Locke claims each has had its day depending on the social environment that was prevalent at the time. Locke dismisses nearly out of hand the first option remarking that many African American artists in the United States have produced the most amateurish works of art due primarily to their poor mastery of African American idioms, and inadequate treatment of African American themes. What is more, some white, or at least non-African American artists, have been quite adept in either their use of characteristically Afrodescendant styles, or their dealings with African American motifs. Of course, it stands to reason that artist stepped in the cultural, ethnic, and racial environments that give rise to these idioms and themes are most likely to master their use and expression, and that persons who do so are most likely to be members of these communities, having the same racial, ethnic or cultural identities as other members. However, such communal membership is not a necessary condition for the work of a particular artist to count among the works that comprise a ethnoracially distinctive body of art such as might be called "African American art." Finally, Locke seems to think the issue of what if anything in American art or culture is distinctively African American somewhat less important and interesting; in the grand scheme of things—because at various points he is extremely concerned with precisely that question—than the issue of how and why African American art and culture are fully American in the broadest sense.

Finally, on Locke's account to be an ethnic race just is to be a variant of a larger culture; there is nothing fundamental, permanent, or essential to ethnic races. To make a contribution to culture is to make a contribution to all humanity. It is to raise something of particular relevance and function beyond its original context to the level of universal human appeal, relevance, and function. All contributions to culture are in the final analysis ethnoracial which is just to specify a kind of particularism out of which cultural products have been crafted. But each in turn transcends that racial or ethnic particularity as it rises from the level of folk expression, to the existential necessity of adaptation and reactive expressive functionality to the heights of excellent and masterful coordination of human sensibilities and expressive potentialities.

IV.   DEMOCRACY'S UNFINISHED BUSINESS

For the same forces which have all but annihilated longitude and latitude also have foreshortened cultural and social distance, and have telescoped their traditional but imaginary dividing lines. Most of all, these new forces for unification are closing in on that great divide of color which so long and so tragically has separated not only East and West, but two thirds of mankind from the other third.

As the new perspective comes into our lives, with its transforming angles of human group relations, we are beginning to sense that we must find common human denominators of liberty, equality and fraternity for *humanity-at-large*. When the democracies in such a crisis ask the world to espouse and defend their cause, they cannot escape the logic by which democracy itself is asked to stretch its tent-ropes to embrace the peoples of the earth. For better or worse, humanity faces the alternatives of world chaos, world tyranny or world order, and must take serious stock of its choices. This is what we presume to call democracy's unfinished business.[131]

Locke's conception of democracy is pervaded by the existential struggles of Afrodescendant peoples to be fully incorporated into the democratic institutions of the cultures they inhabit. The democratic ideal functions in his thought as a stable but evolving standard for measuring a great number of things from the individual attainment of cosmopolitan character to the large-scale realization of a pluralistic and cosmopolitan democratic culture. Locke argues that the proper character is requisite for participation in just institutions as well as the fuller realization of democracy as something more than a political system and set of institutions, but as an increasingly ubiquitous way of life.

Acknowledging his intellectual indebtedness to W.E.B. Du Bois, who famously stated that "The problem of the Twentieth Century would be the problem of the color line,"[132] and connecting his thinking here on democracy with his earlier position on culture and race in connection to democracy, Locke proclaims, that the "[c]rux of this inner conflict is whether our vision of world democracy can clear-sightedly cross the color line, whether we can break through the barriers of cultural racialism to reach the Four Freedoms in their universal goals."[133]

In much the same way that Locke traces the genesis of modern race creeds and practices to the imperial political and economic practices of European nations, he finds that the global practice of colonization has led to a system of "undemocratically related peoples."[134] If the amelioration of undemocratic structures and practices within individual nations required the assertion of a basic equality between persons, Locke reasons that analogously, "the founding of international democracy must guarantee the basic equality of human groups."[135] It follows then, that the continued existence of groups plagued by racial stigmatization, bereft of honor and dignity, and denied political and economic opportunity, runs contrary to the realization of the democratic ideal, and will, wherever it is found, function as a constraint on democratic living. Quite presciently, Locke moves beyond the Inter-American orientation on display in the lectures and articulates a larger postcolonial assessment and critique of existing democracies. He says,

> For those who will boldly look across the new horizons of color today, there is the same logic and the same prophetic vision. They will not find, for example, obvious alignment of the American Negro question with the cause of a free India. Or of Jewry free from cultural disdain and persecution. Or even with the cause of an Africa liberated from colonial exploitation. Or a federated, self-governing Caribbean. Morally, however, there is the closest of connections. For all of these disabilities are part of the same pattern of group relations. In one way or another they involve similar distortions of the democratic principle. Further, they are all justified by rationalizations cut from the same psychological cloth. They are all, as well, items written large on the moral agenda which has become part of the unfinished business of democracy.[136]

Locke contends that the incorporation of African descendant peoples into existing American democracies constitutes a litmus test for gaging the realization of the democratic ideal throughout the Americas, and indeed, around the world. The idea is that the peculiar and ostensible exclusion of African descendant peoples from full and equal participation in democracy provides a measure of just how undemocratic are a given nations practices and institutions. More than that, it makes more transparent the social attitudes and practices that lay back of institutional and legal structures that deny Afrodescendant peoples complete access to political and social life. Yet the importance of African descendant peoples and other persons of color extends well beyond the context of the United States and even the Americas. "For the Negro," Locke contends, "always the test case of the complete internal soundness of our democratic practice, is now a touchstone the world over of our democratic integrity."[137] Locke reasons that the peculiar situation of African descendant peoples throughout the Americas is a paradigm case for analyzing the state of democratic living. An analysis and understanding of the underlying mechanisms through which Afrodescendant peoples are excluded from political, cultural, economic and social participation, yields simultaneously an apprehension of possible means of ameliorative effort aimed at greater possibilities of equality and fraternity.

Following emancipation, Locke claims, "fate cast the Negro in the role of a test case of the basic human right of freedom, of the integrity of our national Constitution, of the Union."[138] Afrodescendant people's role as a standard of evaluation has not always been a marker of failure in American race relations. Often progress on this front has been piecemeal and gradual, and in many instances only coming when it does when forced by the weight of circumstances and unrelenting efforts by Afrodescendant people to problematize white complacency and complicity in an unjust and undemocratic status quo. Even as the condition of African descendant people changes, Locke contends that they remain a crucial indicator of the extent to which liberty and equality are practically and institutionally realized. In part, because wherever they exist in the Americas, Afrodescendant peoples are often highly visible in contrast to their white counterparts, Locke believes they offer a unique opportunity for tracking social progress or regression. Locke writes:

> That our domestic policy of race is a serious impediment in our world relations may well exert unique new pressure as a corrective of traditional American race prejudice. The commitments we have undertaken, the external challenges of the world goals we have set, may well turn out to be the very forces destined to clear our own democracy of its present undemocratic inconsistencies. The more we define this world position and policy, the more paradoxical our race attitudes and traditions will in contrast become. Dictates of expediency may reinforce, at long last, the dictates of conscience.[139]

Within the context of the Americas, and specifically the United States, Locke notes that there is the "perennial hold-over problem of the Negro, her Oriental exclusion dilemma, and other problems of minority attitude that go back even as far as our original bad treatment of the American Indian."[140] As much as Locke is rightly critical of the history of ethnoracial discrimination in the United States, he is equally critical of other parts of the Americas, as when he remarks that "[m]any of the American Republics to the south of us have yet to make the break with labor serfdom and successfully incorporate their aboriginal stocks in the mainstream flow of the national life."[141] There is a price to be paid by continued inattention, or insufficient piecemeal solutions to this problem, or outright intransigence in seeking a solution, in the form of diminishing the faith and morale of subjugated groups within the nation, and further alienating and fueling distrust on the part of potential international allies. "There are persons and interests who," Locke notes, "still think it possible to be halfway democratic in the face of the whole-way demands of the times."[142] He continues that such people "do not see that it is necessary to pluck out from our own body politic all those elements latently or actually of a piece with the creeds and practices of the enemy and all which we externally repudiate and defy."[143]

Locke remarks that the United States having been forced to confront its own racial history in the context of democratic living, and having in many respects considerably more progress to make on that score, is well situated to make a contribution to solving the larger problem of democracy the world over. Also, to its credit, as is the case in many American nations is the widespread diversity within its borders. Locke is at times overly optimistic about the potential of the United States in this regard, but ultimately holds to a sober view which recognizes that "[i]n the neglected and unsolved problem of the Negro in America, the Achilles of the West has a dangerously vulnerable heel."[144] One that, "[a]t any time, in any critical position requiring moral authority before the world ... threatens to impair our influence as an exemplar of democracy."[145] The United States is merely a microcosm of the larger issue, and if only it could perform well under the circumstances it would, in Locke's estimation, gain credibility as a paragon of democratic living, especially among the planet's nonwhite majority.[146]

Importantly, the real issue and problem for democracy is the very concept of racial differentiation and division over and above the particular form that differentiation takes in a given country, or in regard to a specific race. Locke remarks, "color and ethnic differentials correspond very largely to those invidious distinctions between imperial and colonial, dominant and subject status out of which has arisen the double standard of national morality."[147] It seems that for Locke, if racialism is not fundamentally incompatible with full democracy, it is always a potentially obstructing and limiting force. Writing during the course of the Second World War he claims, "[a]s the die is cast, either we are to have forced on us a world of infinitely more racialism or we must ourselves shape a world having infinitely less."[148] Already at the time, Locke sees that "racialism in its new proportions is no longer a minority predicament but now a common danger an imminent majority fate."[149] This is so, not only because of the threat that the Axis Powers pose to the white citizens of the Allied nations but perhaps more significantly because nearly two-thirds of the world's population at the time is nonwhite.

Locke argues that "[t]oday the Negro is cast in an international role involving on a world scale pretty much the same issues of political morality."[150] As it pertains to democracy, the role of African descendant people is not unique, though not for that reason any less important. "The Negro's cause," he argues further, has become "the fulcrum of this extension of democracy, a world hostage to its prospective fulfillment."[151] And though the experiences of African descendant peoples is crucial in this respect, Locke hastens to make clear that it is not the subjugation of a particular race that he is concerned with, but the overall practice of racial differentiation and subjugation itself as a widespread effect of white supremacy. So detrimental is white supremacy to the further development of democracy within nations and around the world, that Locke deems it "[c]rucial in today's situation," that we work toward the postcolonial goal of a "basic readjustment of the status and relationships of the white and non-white peoples, both as peoples of the East and the West and as dominant and subject or colonial peoples."[152] The problem that democracy has yet to confront is not merely the treatment of any specific group of people of color; rather, it is the practice of color differentiation itself with its false creeds and prejudicial practices. He writes: "[c]ertainly here, both nationally and internationally, color becomes the acid test of our fundamental honesty in putting into practice the democracy we preach."[153] Locke concludes from this that "[t]here is essential truth, then, in saying that parity of peoples is the main moral issue of this global conflict."[154]

Locke maintains that squarely confronting the challenge that racialism poses to democracy domestically and internationally is a constructive, rather than, negative response to the problem. "If democracy itself is to survive," he argues, "all the lurking anti-democratic infections in our systems must be discovered and counteracted."[155] And that is the case, "whether manifested in the internal viscera of our nations or as colonial aches and imperial twinges in the farflung extremities of the great world powers."[156] This resonates with the analysis of cultural democracy considered earlier; namely the identification of fundamental barriers to its implementation. Identifying such impediments is not merely a critical exercise; rather it rests on the belief that effective and intelligent ameliorative effort must have the problem it aims to solve clearly in view. That is, one must understand the nature of the problem in terms of it underlying causes and the mechanisms that drive it, as well as its likely consequences.

"Rightly viewed," a nation's own democratic failings "are clues to that equitable reconstruction of group relations so necessary for a truly consistent democracy, so indispensable for a world order of justice and peace."[157] Continuing Locke remarks that "[o]n the list to be renounced, if the new democracy is to be realized, are irresponsible national sovereignty, power politics, military and economic imperialism, racialist notions of world rule and dominance, the persecution of particular minorities, and the bigotry of cultural superiority."[158]

It may seem that Locke underappreciated the degree to which limited democratic achievement would enable the pretense of such moral authority. More than that, he may also seem to have underestimated the extent to which merely formal legal democratic equality would leave unaddressed more systemic forms of denial of democracy in the form of continued unequal education, healthcare, employment opportunities, and voting rights. One should not overstate the case against Locke; he was, in fact, aware of the importance of these domains to the full integration of Afrodescendant people within American democracies. He writes:

> The facilities in existence have never been equal in practice, and therefore the famous formula which promised equality in segregation, proved an illusion. Especially in the economic, but also from the educational point of view, it has never been possible to obtain equal facilities for Whites and Negroes. The organization by the big factories and department stores, of separate Negroes only housing, rendered commercial success impossible despite a few Negro companies. The segregation in housing and schools has always given the Negro poor living conditions and poor conditions of education, without exception, wherever the system was used, whether in the North or in the South .... Yet virtually no Negro authority accepts the principle of segregation, even when forced to resign himself in practice. We can say that segregation is accepted only under duress, but it has never been tolerated and is constantly fought.[159]

In regard to employment, Locke recognizes that "[t]here is growing recognition, particularly among Negroes who were previously apathetic to labor organization because of the labor union policy toward them, that a standardized pay and working conditions spell industrial democracy."[160] Locke noted that "[t]he most potent single factor in this social development of the North American Negro has been an enormous spread and improvement of the Negro press," which has carried out the democratic function of creating conditions so that "the Negro's own attitudes will play an increasing role and have larger effect in the equation of racial adjustment in the United States."[161] Moreover, Locke is certainly attuned to the social changes in the direction of increased democracy that are a consequence of American participation in the Second World War. He notes that "in previously barred or limited branches of military service, the Navy, the Marine Corps and military aviation, extensions of Negro eligibility and participation have been put in force, much of it on the initiative and pressure of Negro public opinion."[162] But more to the point, Locke's prescience on this point enables him to see that "[t]hese considerable contingents will return not only deserving more of our democracy but expecting more, and it is idle to think that in a democratic system this will not have revolutionizing effect."[163] Locke observes a general trend toward bi-racially cooperative social action on multiple fronts; "[t]his approach also links up the effort to benefit the Negro and right his group injustices with all the national campaigns for practical and progressive democracy, such as the movements for better popular education, wider use of the franchise, labor rights, social security, farm reconstruction, civic improvement of sub-standard housing and living generally."[164]

V.   CONCLUSION

A representation of the content of the lectures is not the aim of this essay, to that end, the lectures have been allowed, in some sense, to stand on their own. Instead, what is offered here is a thematic attempt to systematize important, fundamental, and characteristic features of Locke's philosophical worldview, which includes inter alia Locke's philosophy of race, culture and democracy, and his understanding of specifically Afrodescendant ethnoracial contributions to the Americas' cultures, and the underlying methodological frameworks of critical pragmatism and Inter-American philosophy. Over the course of the lecture series, Locke makes use of his critical pragmatism to lay a philosophical foundation for an Inter-American methodology and framework for comprehending the various roles of African descendant peoples in the Americas' cultures. Moreover, Locke makes a compelling case for the practical necessity of making use of that framework as a means of reorienting present philosophical concerns toward the realization of cultural democracy and pluralism. It is to be hoped that contemporary scholars will find in these lectures and accompanying interpretive essay a philosophically fecund examination of African cultural contributions throughout the Americas, minority representation and marginalization in democratic contexts, the ethics of racial representation, the notion of cultural transformation and transparency, a critical and prescient analysis of ethnic race and culture, and the ethical issues involved in cross-cultural exchanges. Effort has been made to lay bare the philosophical significance of the works anthologized, and the significance of these works for various contemporary philosophical discourses, as well as debates in cultural anthropology, history, African- and Latin American studies, literary theory, and art history. Beyond a careful display of the continued relevance of Locke's work, and the indispensability of his contribution to critical cultural studies, Locke seeks to problematize the hegemonic theorization of the Americas from the vantage point of the United States. He does, of course, pay attention to the United States, and in point of fact, three of the six lectures are explicitly concerned with the United States, but even in those instances the driving motivation is to make African Americans in the United States better known and more thoroughly understood in other parts of the diaspora and further abroad. Also, as Locke understands it, Afrodescendant people in the United States can serve as a useful test case for a consideration of the broader philosophical themes he addresses throughout the essays. Moreover, acknowledges that that is not a role to be played exclusively by African descendant people in the United States, as many other Afrodescendant populations, and non-Afrodescendant groups such as indigenous populations, in the Americas can be used to similar effect. It is one of Locke's aims to make conceptions of pragmatism, and (Inter-) American philosophy, more expansive and representative of the philosophical endeavors of various American peoples than do prevailing trends; as he attempts to come to sober theoretical and practical terms with the difficulties and possibilities of bridging diverse cultures.

It has been necessary for seeking to properly contextualize the lectures in Locke's overall philosophy to supplement a careful interpretation of them with an exegesis of previously published work that helps to contextualize the lectures. To that end, care has been taken to flesh out in a critical and accessible manner the important concepts, arguments, and themes contained in the lectures. Possibly, this will make the texts less avoidable for scholars interested in studying the intersections of various traditions in American philosophy. It is that novel perspective and the relative dearth of present scholarship in pursuit of that aim that gives the work its greatest chance of impacting contemporary scholarship by initiating new avenues of study and shifting existing avenues into new directions.

It is a largely unknown, and in circles where it is discussed, underappreciated and misunderstood, aspect of Locke's philosophy of race that it entails a form of racial eliminativism. It is a matter of some controversy exactly what form that eliminativism takes.[165] Locke radically reconceives race in contrast to the views prevalent during his day. So fundamental in fact is his revised understanding of race that where he ends up with the concept of ethnic race, is a phenomenon quite unlike what many contemporary philosophers of race have in mind. When that reconceptualization, is substituted for contemporary conceptualizations as Locke argues it should be, the result is tantamount to an elimination of the former conception. This is a fact about Locke's philosophy that has failed to be fully understood and appreciated by scholars of his work and others working in closely aligned fields. It seems that race, in Locke's view, is culture: or conversely, that culture is race. That is, what race comes to in his view, is a particular subcultural variant, relatively understood, impermanent, transactional in constitution, and inherently transformational, with nothing in the way of biological determinants fixing the categories.

Culture, for Locke, is a dynamic medium of interaction in a constant state of transformation. It is the medium through which human beings live, create meaning, structure lives, and create the conditions for their flourishing. Locke argued throughout his career for a relative understanding of cultures and a commitment to an acknowledged parity between cultures.[166] These are crucial elements that underlie the concept of cultural pluralism. Locke further argued against the idea of cultural proprietorship; that is, the belief that a dominant ethnoracial group is the singular source of cultural productions and contributions, or the conviction that persons with a given ethnoracial identity have privileged access to membership in a culture, and the sole rights to use of that culture as artistic source material. Cultures, for Locke, are composite and transformational, and their products belong to all of humanity. Racial contributions to culture are then a set of composite cultural products and influences with pluralistic origins in terms of authorship that make use of a relatively discernable culture-type situated within a larger shared cultural context. As such, Locke regards them as a genuine feature of American culture in the USA. Locke's commitment to cultural pluralism and parity, and his rejection of cultural proprietorship result in an open-ended appreciation of cultural participation. He argued for the importance of making access to culture open, free, and equitable.

Cultural democracy is an important pragmatic ideal that runs throughout many aspects of Locke's philosophy. It is no accident that Locke begins his lectures in Haiti with a careful examination of this concept in an Inter-American context. Locke's cosmopolitan orientation and commitment to cultural pluralism began as early as his time at Oxford as a Rhodes scholar. He continued to develop these positions until they matured into a philosophical understanding of cultural democracy on a global scale. In this regard, these lectures constitute a quintessential statement of Locke's philosophy. That this crucial statement came in the form of a series of lectures may have hampered the extent to which he was able to shape contemporary philosophical discourse on the subjects he addresses in the lectures. That situation has here been remedied. What remains to be seen is the response of contemporary scholars concerned with these issues.

NOTES

1. Kadlec, Alison. "Reconstructing Dewey: The Philosophy of Critical Pragmatism." *Polity* 38, 4, (2006): 519–542.
2. Kadlec, "Reconstructing Dewey," 522.
3. Locke, "The Negro in the Three Americas," *The Journal of Negro Education* 13:1 (1944): 7–18. 11–12.
4. Locke, "Race, Culture and Democracy," 1943, Box 164–126, Folder 4, Alain Locke Papers Howard University (Hereafter ALPHU), Manuscript Division, Founders Library, Howard University, Washington, DC.
5. Locke, "Race, Culture and Democracy," ALPHU, 164–126, 4.
6. Locke, "Race, Culture and Democracy," ALPHU, 164–126, 4.
7. Locke, "The Negro in the Three Americas," 18.
8. Locke, "The Negro in the Three Americas," 11.
9. Locke, "The Negro in the Three Americas," 9.
10. Locke, "The Negro in the Three Americas," 9.
11. Locke, "Race, Culture and Democracy," ALPHU, 164–126, 4.
12. Locke, "Race, Culture and Democracy," ALPHU, 164–126, 4.
13. Locke, "Race, Culture and Democracy," ALPHU, 164–126, 4.
14. Locke, "Race, Culture and Democracy," ALPHU, 164–126, 4.
15. Locke, "Race, Culture and Democracy," ALPHU, 164–126, 4.
16. Locke, "Race, Culture and Democracy," ALPHU, 164–126, 4.
17. Locke, Alain. "The Contribution of Race to Culture," in *The Philosophy of Alain Locke: Harlem Renaissance and Beyond*, edited by Leonard Harris, 202–206. Philadelphia: Temple University Press, 1989. 204.

18. Alain Leroy Locke, *Race Contacts and Interracial Relations: Lectures in the Theory and Practice of Race*. Edited by Jeffrey C. Stewart. Washington, DC: Howard University Press, 1992.
19. Alain Leroy Locke, "The Concept of Race as Applied to Social Culture," in *The Critical Temper of Alain Locke: A Selection of His Essays on Art and Culture*, edited by Jeffrey C. Stewart, 423–429.
20. Alain Leroy Locke, "The Concept of Race as Applied to Social Culture," in *The Philosophy of Alain Locke: Harlem Renaissance and Beyond*, edited by Leonard Harris, 188–199. Philadelphia: Temple University Press, 1989. 188.
21. Locke, "The Concept of Race as Applied to Social Culture," 188.
22. Locke, "The Concept of Race as Applied to Social Culture," 188.
23. Locke, "The Concept of Race as Applied to Social Culture," 189.
24. Locke, "The Concept of Race as Applied to Social Culture," 189.
25. Locke, "The Concept of Race as Applied to Social Culture," 189.
26. Locke, "The Concept of Race as Applied to Social Culture," 189.
27. Locke, "The Concept of Race as Applied to Social Culture," 189.
28. Locke, "The Concept of Race as Applied to Social Culture," 189.
29. Locke, "The Concept of Race as Applied to Social Culture," 190.
30. Locke, "The Concept of Race as Applied to Social Culture," 194.
31. Locke, "The Concept of Race as Applied to Social Culture," 194.
32. Locke, "The Concept of Race as Applied to Social Culture," 194.
33. Locke, "The Concept of Race as Applied to Social Culture," 194.
34. Locke, "The Concept of Race as Applied to Social Culture," 194.
35. Locke, "The Concept of Race as Applied to Social Culture," 191.
36. Locke, "The Concept of Race as Applied to Social Culture," 191.
37. Locke, "The Concept of Race as Applied to Social Culture," 192.
38. Locke, "The Concept of Race as Applied to Social Culture," 192.
39. Locke, "The Concept of Race as Applied to Social Culture," 193.
40. Locke, "The Concept of Race as Applied to Social Culture," 192.
41. Locke, "The Concept of Race as Applied to Social Culture," 192.
42. Locke, "The Concept of Race as Applied to Social Culture," 190.
43. Locke, "The Concept of Race as Applied to Social Culture," 190.
44. Locke, "The Concept of Race as Applied to Social Culture," 190.
45. Locke, "The Concept of Race as Applied to Social Culture," 190–191.
46. Locke, "The Concept of Race as Applied to Social Culture," 195.
47. Locke, "The Concept of Race as Applied to Social Culture," 196.
48. Locke, "The Concept of Race as Applied to Social Culture," 196.

49. Locke, "The Concept of Race as Applied to Social Culture," 197–198.
50. Alain Leroy Locke, *Race Contacts and Interracial Relations: Lectures in the Theory and Practice of Race*. Edited by Jeffrey C. Stewart. Washington, DC: Howard University Press. 1992. 63.
51. Locke, *Race Contacts and Interracial Relations*, 63–64.
52. Locke, *Race Contacts and Interracial Relations*, 22–23.
53. Locke, *Race Contacts and Interracial Relations*, 28.
54. Locke, *Race Contacts and Interracial Relations*, 29.
55. Locke, *Race Contacts and Interracial Relations*, 22.
56. Locke, *Race Contacts and Interracial Relations*, 22.
57. Alain Leroy Locke, "The Contribution of Race to Culture," in *The Philosophy of Alain Locke: Harlem Renaissance and Beyond*, edited by Leonard Harris, 202–206. Philadelphia: Temple University Press, 1989.
58. Locke, "The Contribution of Race to Culture," 203.
59. Martí, José. "My Race," in *José Martí: Selected Writings*, translated by Esther Allen. New York: Penguin, 2002. 318–321.
60. Martí, "My Race," 319.
61. Martí, "My Race," 319.
62. Locke, "The Contribution of Race to Culture," 202–203.
63. Locke, "Frontiers of Culture," in *The Philosophy of Alain Locke: Harlem Renaissance and Beyond*, edited by Leonard Harris, 230–236. Philadelphia: Temple University Press, 1989. 236.
64. Locke, "Frontiers of Culture," 236.
65. Locke, "The Ethics of Culture," in *The Philosophy of Alain Locke: Harlem Renaissance and Beyond*, edited by Leonard Harris, 176–185. Philadelphia: Temple University Press, 1989. 180.
66. Locke, "The Ethics of Culture," 177.
67. Locke, "The Ethics of Culture," 177.
68. Locke, "The Ethics of Culture," 177.
69. See, for example, Dewey, John. Freedom and Culture. In The Later Works of John Dewey, Volume 13, 1925–1953: 1938–1939, edited by Jo Ann Boydston, Carbondale: Southern Illinois University Press, 2008.
70. Locke, "The Ethics of Culture," 177.
71. Locke, "The Ethics of Culture," 177.
72. Locke, "The Ethics of Culture," 177–178.

73. Alain Leroy Locke, "Race, Culture and Democracy," 1943, Box 164–126, Folder 4, Alain Locke Papers Howard University (Hereafter ALPHU), Manuscript Division, Founders Library, Howard University, Washington, DC.
74. Locke, "Race, Culture and Democracy," ALPHU, 164–126, 4.
75. Locke, "Race, Culture and Democracy," ALPHU, 164–126, 4.
76. Locke, "Race, Culture and Democracy," ALPHU, 164–126, 4.
77. Locke, "Race, Culture and Democracy," ALPHU, 164–126, 4.
78. Locke, "Frontiers of Culture," 233–234.
79. Locke, "Race, Culture and Democracy," ALPHU, 164–126, 4.
80. Locke, "Pluralism and Intellectual Democracy," in *The Philosophy of Alain Locke: Harlem Renaissance and Beyond*, edited by Leonard Harris. Philadelphia: Temple University Press, 1989. 55. For a more thorough discussion of Locke's axiology, specifically the notions of basic equivalence and functional equivalence see "Values and Imperatives," "Cultural Relativism and Ideological Peace," and "A Functional View of Value Ultimates," in *The Philosophy of Alain Locke: Harlem Renaissance and Beyond*, edited by Leonard Harris, Philadelphia: Temple University Press, 1989. See also, "New Moral Imperatives for World Order: Alain Locke's Pluralism and Relativism," in *Philosophic Values and World Citizenship: Locke to Obama and Beyond*, edited by Jacoby Adeshei Carter and Leonard Harris, Lexington: Lexington Books Press, 2010, or "Alain LeRoy Locke" in *Stanford Encyclopedia of Philosophy* (Summer 2012), Edward N. Zalta (ed.), URL =<http://plato.stanford.edu/archives/sum2012/entries/alain-locke/>.
81. Locke, "Frontiers of Culture," 233.
82. Locke, "Race, Culture and Democracy," ALPHU, 164–126, 4.
83. Locke, "Race, Culture and Democracy," ALPHU, 164–126, 4.
84. Locke, "Race, Culture and Democracy," ALPHU, 164–126, 4.
85. Locke, "Race, Culture and Democracy," ALPHU, 164–126, 4.
86. Locke, "Frontiers of Culture," 233.
87. Alain Leroy Locke, "The Negro's Contribution to American Art and Literature," *The Annals of the American Academy*, (1928): 140, 234–247.
88. Alain Leroy Locke, "The Negro's Contribution to American Art and Literature," *Annals of the American Academy of Political and Social Science*, (1928), 140, 234–247. 234.

89. Locke, "The Negro's Contribution to American Art and Literature," 234.
90. Locke, "The Negro's Contribution to American Art and Literature," 234.
91. Locke, "The Negro's Contribution to American Art and Literature," 234.
92. Locke, "The African Heritage and Its Cultural Significance," ALPHU, 164–126, 6 and 7.
93. Locke, "The Negro's Contribution to American Art and Literature," 234.
94. Alain Leroy Locke, "Cultural Relativism and Ideological Peace," in *The Philosophy of Alain Locke: Harlem Renaissance and Beyond*, edited by Leonard Harris, 69–78. Philadelphia: Temple University Press, 1989. 73.
95. Locke, "The Negro's Contribution to American Art and Literature," 234–235.
96. Locke, "The Negro's Contribution to American Art and Literature," 235.
97. Locke, "The Negro's Contribution to American Art and Literature," 236.
98. Locke, "The Negro's Contribution to American Art and Literature," 237.
99. Locke, "The Negro's Contribution to American Art and Literature," 237.
100. Locke, "The Negro's Contribution to American Art and Literature," 237.
101. David Walker, *Appeal in Four Articles to the Colored Citizens of the World*, University Park: Penn State University Press, 2000.
102. Locke, "The Negro's Contribution to American Art and Literature," 238.
103. Locke, "The Negro's Contribution to American Art and Literature," 238.
104. Locke, "The Negro's Contribution to American Art and Literature," 238.
105. Locke, "The Negro's Contribution to American Art and Literature," 238–239.
106. Locke, "The Negro's Contribution to American Art and Literature," 239.

107. Locke, "The Negro's Contribution to American Art and Literature," 239.

108. Locke, "The Negro's Contribution to American Art and Literature," 239.

109. Locke, "The Negro's Contribution to American Art and Literature," 239.

110. Locke, "The Negro's Contribution to American Art and Literature," 240.

111. Locke, "The Negro's Contribution to American Art and Literature," 241.

112. Locke, "The Negro's Contribution to American Art and Literature," 242.

113. Locke, "The Negro's Contribution to American Art and Literature," 242.

114. Locke, "The Negro's Contribution to American Art and Literature," 242.

115. Locke, "The Negro's Contribution to American Art and Literature," 242.

116. Locke, "The Negro's Contribution to American Art and Literature," 242.

117. Locke, "The Negro's Contribution to American Art and Literature," 244.

118. Locke, "The Negro's Contribution to American Art and Literature," 244.

119. Alain Leroy Locke, "The Negro's Contribution to American Culture," *The Journal of Negro Education*, (1939), 8:3, 521–529. 521.

120. Alain Leroy Locke, "Who and What is Negro?" in *The Philosophy of Alain Locke: Harlem Renaissance and Beyond*, edited by Leonard Harris, 209–228. Philadelphia: Temple University Press, 1989.

121. Locke, "The Negro's Contribution to American Culture," 521.

122. Locke, "The Negro's Contribution to American Culture," 522.

123. Locke, "The Negro's Contribution to American Culture," 522.

124. Locke, "The Negro's Contribution to American Culture," 522.

125. Locke, "The Negro's Contribution to American Culture," 522.

126. Locke, "The Negro's Contribution to American Culture," 521–522.

127. Locke, "The Negro's Contribution to American Culture," 522.

128. Locke, "Who and What is Negro?" 209.

129. Locke, "Who and What is Negro?" 210.
130. Locke, "Who and What is Negro?" 211.
131. Locke, Alain. "The Unfinished Business of Democracy," Survey Graphic: Magazine of Social Interpretation, (1942), 31:11, 455–461.
132. Du Bois, W. E. B., *The Souls of Black Folk*, New York: Dover Publications, 1994. v.
133. Locke, "The Unfinished Business of Democracy," 456.
134. Locke, "The Unfinished Business of Democracy," 456.
135. Locke, "The Unfinished Business of Democracy," 456.
136. Locke, "The Unfinished Business of Democracy," 456.
137. Locke, "The Unfinished Business of Democracy," 458.
138. Locke, "The Unfinished Business of Democracy," 459.
139. Locke, "The Unfinished Business of Democracy," 458–459.
140. Locke, "The Unfinished Business of Democracy," 457.
141. Locke, "The Unfinished Business of Democracy," 457.
142. Locke, "The Unfinished Business of Democracy," 457.
143. Locke, "The Unfinished Business of Democracy," 457.
144. Locke, "The Unfinished Business of Democracy," 458.
145. Locke, "The Unfinished Business of Democracy," 458.
146. Locke, "The Unfinished Business of Democracy," 458.
147. Locke, Alain. "The Unfinished Business of Democracy," *Survey Graphic: Magazine of Social Interpretation*, (1942), 31:11, 455–461.
148. Locke, "The Unfinished Business of Democracy," 456.
149. Locke, "The Unfinished Business of Democracy," 457.
150. Locke, "The Unfinished Business of Democracy," 459.
151. Locke, "The Unfinished Business of Democracy," 459.
152. Locke, "The Unfinished Business of Democracy," 456.
153. Locke, "The Unfinished Business of Democracy," 456.
154. Locke, "The Unfinished Business of Democracy," 456.
155. Locke, "The Unfinished Business of Democracy," 457.
156. Locke, "The Unfinished Business of Democracy," 457.
157. Locke, "The Unfinished Business of Democracy," 458.
158. Locke, "The Unfinished Business of Democracy," 458.
159. Locke, "The Negro's Sociological Position in the United States," ALPHU, 164–126, 14.
160. Locke, "The Negro's Sociological Position in the United States," ALPHU, 164–126, 14.

161. Locke, "The Negro's Sociological Position in the United States," ALPHU, 164–126, 14.
162. Locke, "The Negro's Sociological Position in the United States," ALPHU, 164–126, 14.
163. Locke, "The Negro's Sociological Position in the United States," ALPHU, 164–126, 14.
164. Locke, "The Negro's Sociological Position in the United States," ALPHU, 164–126, 14.
165. See Jacoby Adeshei Carter, "Between Reconstruction and Eliminativism: Alain Locke's Philosophy of Race," in *The Oxford Handbook on Philosophy and Race*, edited by Naomi Zack, forthcoming.
166. See Locke, "Cultural Relativism and Ideological Peace," 71–75.

BIBLIOGRAPHY

Allahar, Anton, ed. 2005. *Ethnicity, Class, and Nationalism: Caribbean and Extra-Caribbean Dimensions*. Lanham: Lexington Books.

Bernstein, Richard J. 2015. Cultural Pluralism. *Philosophy & Social Criticism* 41(4): 347–356.

Branche, Jerome, ed. 2008. *Race, Colonialism, and Social Transformation in Latin America and the Caribbean*. Gainesville: University Press of Florida.

Butcher, Margaret Just. 1956. *The Negro in American Culture*. New York: Knopf.

Carter, Jacoby A., and Leonard Harris, eds. 2010. *Philosophic Values and World Citizenship: Locke to Obama and Beyond*. Lexington: Lexington Books Press.

Carter, Jacoby A. 2012. Alain LeRoy Locke. In *Stanford Encyclopedia of Philosophy*, ed. Edward N. Zalta. http://plato.stanford.edu/archives/sum2012/entries/alain-locke/

———. 2013. The Insurrectionist Challenge to Pragmatism and Maria W. Stewart's Feminist Insurrectionist Ethics. *Transactions of the Charles S. Pierce Society* 49(1): 54–73.

———. 2014. Does "Race" Have a Future or Should the Future Have "Races"? Reconstruction or Eliminativism in a Pragmatist Philosophy of Race. *Transactions of the Charles S. Pierce Society* 50(1): 29–47.

———. forthcoming. Between Reconstruction and Eliminativism: Alain Locke's Philosophy of Race. In *The Oxford Handbook on Philosophy and Race*, ed. Naomi Zack. New York: Oxford University Press.

Curry, Tommy J. 2007. Who K(new): The Nation-ist Contour of Racial Identity in the Thought of Martin R. Delany and John E. Bruce. *Journal of Pan-African Studies* 1(10): 41–61.

© The Editor(s) (if applicable) and The Author(s) 2016
J.A. Carter, *African American Contributions to the Americas' Cultures*, DOI 10.1057/978-1-137-56572-3

————. 2010. Concerning the Under-specialization of Race Theory in American Philosophy: An Essay Outlining Ignored Bibliographic Sources Addressing the Aforementioned Problem. *The Pluralist* 5(1): 44–64.

————. 2011a. The Derelictical Crisis of African American Philosophy: How African American Philosophy Fails to Contribute to the Study of African Descended People. *Journal of Black Studies* 42(3): 314–333.

————. 2011b. On Derelict and Method: The Methodological Crisis of Africana Philosophy's Study of African Descended People Under an Integrationist Milieu. *Radical Philosophy Review* 14(2): 139–164.

————. 2012. The Fortune of Wells: Ida B. Wells-Barnett's Use of T. Thomas Fortune Philosophy of Social Agitation as a Prolegomenon to Militant Civil Rights Activism. *Transactions of the Charles S. Pierce Society* 48(8): 456–482.

Demenchonok, Edward. 2005. Intercultural Discourse and African-Caribbean Philosophy. *Dialogue & Universalism* 15(1): 181–201.

Dewey, John. 2008. *Freedom and Culture*. In *The Later Works of John Dewey, Volume 13, 1925–1953: 1938–1939*, ed. Jo Ann Boydston. Carbondale: Southern Illinois University Press.

Du Bois, William Edward Burghardt. 1994. *The Souls of Black Folk*. New York: Dover Publications.

Firmin, Anténor. 2002. *The Equality of the Human Races*, Trans. Asselin Charles. Urbana: University of Illinois Press.

Gogol, Eugene. 2002. *The Concept of Other in Latin American Liberation: Fusing Emancipatory Philosophic Thought and Social Revolt*. Lanham: Lexington Books.

Goodin, Patrick L. 2000. On the very Idea of an Afro-Caribbeana Philosophy. *African Philosophy* 13(2): 143–152.

Gordon, Lewis R. 2008. *An Introduction to Africana Philosophy*. New York: Cambridge University Press.

Gracia, Jorge J.E., and Elizabeth Millán-Zaibert, eds. 2004. *Latin American Philosophy for the 21st Century: The Human Condition, Values, and the Search for Identity*. Amherst: Prometheus Books.

Haile, James B. III. 2015. The Cultural-Logic Turn of Black Philosophy. *Radical Philosophy Review* 18(1): 129–150.

Harris, Leonard, ed. 1984. *Philosophy Born of Struggle: Afro-American Philosophy from 1917*. Iowa: Kendall Hunt Publishing Company.

————. 1987. The Legitimation Crisis in American Philosophy: Crisis Resolution from the Standpoint of the Afro-American Tradition of Philosophy. *Social Science Information* 21(1): 57–73.

————. 1988a. The Characterization of American Philosophy: The African World as a Reality in American Philosophy. *Quest: Philosophical Discussions* 11(1): 25–36.

————. 1988b. Identity: Alain Locke's Atavism. *Transactions of the Charles S. Peirce Society* 26(1): 65–84.

————. 1989a. The Lacuna Between Philosophy and History. *The Journal of Social Philosophy* 20(3): 110–114.

————. 1989b. *The Philosophy of Alain Locke: Harlem Renaissance and Beyond.* Philadelphia: Temple University Press.

————. 1991. Columbus and the Identity of the Americas. *Annals of Scholarship* 8(2): 287–299.

————. 1998. The Concept of Racism: An Essentially Contested Concept? *Centennial Review* 42(2): 217–232.

————, ed. 1999a. *The Critical Pragmatism of Alain Locke: A Reader on Value Theory, Aesthetics, Community, Culture, Race, and Education.* Lanham: Rowman & Littlefield.

————, ed. 1999b. *Racism.* New York: Humanity Press.

————. 1999c. Alain Locke and Community. *Journal of Ethics* 1: 1–9.

————. 2002. Insurrectionist Ethics: Advocacy, Moral Psychology, and Pragmatism. In *Ethical Issues for a New Millennium: The Wayne Leys Memorial Lectures,* ed. John Howie, 192–210. Carbondale: Southern Illinois University Press.

————. 2004. The Great Debate: Alain L. Locke vs. W.E.B. Du Bois. *Philosophia Africana* 7(1): 13–37.

————. 2009. Cosmopolitanism and the African Renaissance: Pixley I. Seme and Alain L. Locke. *International Journal of African Renaissance Studies* 4(2): 181–192.

————. 2012. Against Minstrelsy. *Black Diaspora Review* 3(2): 1–13.

————. 2013. Walker: Naturalism and Liberation. *Transactions of the C. S. Peirce Society* 49(1): 93–111.

————. 2014. Philosophy of Philosophy: Race, Nation and Religion. *Graduate Journal of Philosophy* 35(1): 1–12.

Harris, Leonard, and Charles Molesworth. 2010. *Alain L. Locke: Biography of a Philosopher.* Chicago: University of Chicago Press.

Harris, Leonard, Scott L. Pratt, and Anne Waters, eds. 2002. *American Philosophies.* Oxford: Blackwell Publishing Company.

James, C.L.R. 1989. *The Black Jacobins: Toussaint L'Ouverture and the San Domingo Revolution.* New York: Vintage Books.

Linnemann, Russell J., ed. 1982. *Alain Locke: Reflections on a Modern Renaissance Man.* Baton Rouge: Louisiana State University Press.

Locke, Alain LeRoy, ed. 1927. *Four Negro Poets.* New York: Simon & Schuster.

————, ed. 1936. *Negro Art: Past and Present.* Washington, DC: Associates in Negro Folk Education.

————, ed. 1942a. Color: Unfinished Business of Democracy. *Survey Graphic: Magazine of Social Interpretation,* 31(11): 455–461.

————. 1943. *The Negro's Contribution to the Culture of the Americas,* Box 164–126, Folder 4–29, Alain Locke Papers Howard University Manuscript Division, Founders Library, Howard University, Washington, DC.

————, ed. 1969. *The Negro and His Music.* New York: Arno Press.

————, ed. 1971. *The Negro in Art: A Pictorial Record of the Negro Artist and of the Negro Theme in Art.* New York: Hacker Art Books.

————, ed. 1999. *The New Negro: Voices from the Harlem Renaissance.* New York: Simon & Schuster.

Locke, Alain. 1924. The Concept of Race as Applied to Social Culture. *Howard Review* 1: 290–299.

————. 1928. The Negro's Contribution to American Art and Literature. *The Annals of the American Academy of Political and Social Science* 140: 234–247.

————. 1939. The Negro's Contribution to American Culture. *The Journal of Negro Education* 8(3): 521–529.

————. 1942b. The Unfinished Business of Democracy. *Survey Graphic: Magazine of Social Interpretation* 31(11): 455–461.

————. 1944. The Negro in the Three Americas. *The Journal of Negro Education* 13(1): 7–18.

————. 1946. The Negro Minority in American Literature. *The English Journal* 35(6): 315–320.

Locke, Alain LeRoy, and Bernhard Joseph Stern, eds. 1946. *When Peoples Meet: A Study in Race and Culture Contacts.* New York: Hinds, Hayden & Eldredge.

Macmullan, Terance. 2005. Challenges to Cultural Diversity: Absolutism, Democracy, and Alain Locke's Value Relativism. *Journal of Speculative Philosophy* 19(2): 129–139.

Maldonado-Torres, Nelson. 2003. Walking to the Fourth World of the Caribbean. *Nepantla: Views from South* 4(3): 561–565.

Martí, José. 2002. *José Martí: Selected Writings.* Trans. Esther Allen. New York: Penguin.

McBride, Lee. 2012. Agrarian Ideals and Practices: Comments on Paul B. Thompson's The Agrarian Vision. *Journal of Agricultural and Environmental Ethics* 25(4): 535–541.

————. 2013a. Insurrectionist Ethics and Thoreau. *Transactions of the Charles S. Peirce Society* 49(1): 29–45.

———— (ed). 2013b. Symposium on Insurrectionist Ethics. *Transactions of the Charles S. Peirce Society* 49(1): 27–111.

————. 2016. Insurrectionist Ethics and Racism. In *The Oxford Handbook of Philosophy and Race*, ed. Naomi Zack. New York: Oxford University Press.

————. forthcoming. Racial Imperialism and Food Traditions. In *The Oxford Handbook of Food Ethics*, ed. Tyler Doggett, Anne Barnhill, and Mark Budolfson. New York: Oxford University Press.

Medina, José. 2004. Pragmatism and Ethnicity: Critique, Reconstruction, and the New Hispanic. *Metaphilosophy* 35(1): 115–146.

————. 2009. Whose Meanings?: Resignifying Voices and their Social Locations. *The Journal of Speculative Philosophy* 22(2): 92–105.

Mendoza, J. 2011. Does "Sí Se Puede" Translate To "Yes We Can"? *Philosophy in the Contemporary World* 18(2): 60–69.

———. 2012. Immigration: The Missing Requirement for an Ethics of Race. *Radical Philosophy Review* 15(2): 359–364.

———. 2015. Does Cosmopolitan Justice Ever Require Restrictions on Migration? *Public Affairs Quarterly* 29(2): 175–187.

Mendieta, Eduardo, ed. 2003. *Latin American Philosophy: Currents, Issues, Debates*. Bloomington, IN: Indiana University Press.

———. 2007. *Global Fragments: Latinamericanisms, Globalizations and Critical Theory*. Albany: State University of New York Press.

———. 2011. Pragmatism and the Ethics of Global Citizenship: Latinos and Transnationalism. *Inter-American Journal of Philosophy* 2(1): 26–34.

Millan-Zaibert, Elizabeth, and Arleen L.F. Salles, eds. 2005. *The Role of History in Latin American Philosophy: Contemporary Perspectives*. Albany: State University of New York Press.

Moreira, Luiza Franco. 2012. Songs and Intellectuals: The Musical Projects of Alain Locke, Alejo Carpentier, and Mário De Andrade. *Comparative Literature Studies* 49(2): 210–226.

Nuccetelli, Susana, and Gary Seay, eds. 2004. *Latin American Philosophy: An Introduction with Readings*. Upper Saddle River, NJ: Prentice Hall.

Pappas, Gregory Fernando, ed. 2011. *Pragmatism in the Americas*. New York: Fordham University Press.

Roberts, Neil. 2015. *Freedom as Marronage*. Chicago: University of Chicago Press.

Scott, David. 2004. *Conscripts of Modernity: The Tragedy of Colonial Enlightenment*. Durham: Duke University Press.

Stewart, Jeffrey C., ed. 1983. *The Critical Temper of Alain Locke: A Selection of His Essays on Art and Culture*. New York: Garland Pub.

———, ed. 1992. *Race Contacts and Interracial Relations: Lectures in the Theory and Practice of Race*. Washington, DC: Howard University Press.

Vest, Jennifer Lisa. 2005. The Promise of Caribbean Philosophy: How It Can Contribute to a 'New dialogic' in Philosophy. *Caribbean Studies* 33(2): 3–34.

Walker, David. 2000. *Appeal in Four Articles to the Colored Citizens of the World*. University Park: Penn State University Press.

White, Morton Gabriel. 1973. *Pragmatism and the American Mind: Essays and Reviews in Philosophy and Intellectual History*. New York: Oxford University Press.

Wilson, Elvinet S. 2009. What it Means to Become a United States American: Afro-Caribbean Immigrants' Constructions of American Citizenship and Experience of Cultural Transition. *Journal of Ethnographic & Qualitative Research* 3(3): 196–204.

Wright, Louis E. 2011. Alain Locke on Race Relations: Some Political Implications of His Thought. *Journal of Black Studies* 42(4): 665–689.

Index

© The Editor(s) (if applicable) and The Author(s) 2016
J.A. Carter, *African American Contributions to the Americas' Cultures*, DOI 10.1057/978-1-137-56572-3